"Many preachers in the early twenty-first century are vexed by the current vortex of postmodernism, the pandemic, digital media, artificial intelligence, and political partisanship in the churches. Casey Sigmon gives us the first book that makes a theological appraisal of this situation and that offers local preachers practical ways to navigate it. Like its title, the book itself is a gadfly whose friendly bite will stimulate creative responses."

—RONALD J. ALLEN,
professor emeritus of preaching, and of gospels and letters, Christian Theological Seminary, Indianapolis

"The digital age is here to stay! Our approaches to worship and preaching must adapt to the new tools and the new contexts that have emerged since 2020. This does not mean that traditional worship spaces are on the way out, nor does it mean that digital worship and preaching will continue functioning as an appendage. The Spirit is guiding the church in innovative and collaborative ways, if we will follow the Spirit's lead. Casey Sigmon presents a prophetic call to follow the creative force being unleashed by the Spirit. While many of us have offered practical approaches for engaging in digital preaching and worship, Casey offers us what we have been lacking—the theological groundwork to build on. Her concept of 'homilecclesiology' is nothing short of pastoral genius, imagined by one who believes deeply in preaching and exudes creativity. I am blessed to call Casey a friend and believe firmly that this book will guide our conversations for years to come."

—ROB O'LYNN,
associate professor of preaching and ministry, Kentucky Christian University

"*Engaging the Gadfly* shatters the boundaries of traditional preaching, pushing us into the exhilarating, uncharted territory of digital ministry. Casey T. Sigmon delivers a revolutionary approach to homiletics, empowering pastors to disrupt the status quo and embrace the chaos of the digital age. If you're ready to step out of your comfort zone and radically transform how you preach, this book is your blueprint for the future."

—SUNGGU A. YANG,
associate professor of theology and Christian ministries,
George Fox University

"*Engaging the Gadfly* calls us to consider preaching that attends to the possibilities of technology from a place of depth. It is practical theology at its best—bridging theory and practice so that readers are given the *what* and *why* in order to move towards the *how* more effectively. With wit and innovation, this text is excellent for all preachers who proclaim within the expansive possibilities of technoculture—which in this age is all preachers.

—CHELSEA BROOKE YARBOROUGH,
associate director of leadership programming,
Association of Theological Schools

"With wit and candor, Dr. Sigmon encourages preachers to expand their understanding not just of what preaching should be, but what it should *do*. As has been true throughout history, a new era of technology is a chance for the church to reexamine its means *and* its ends—not as a navel-gazing exercise, but to discover the unfolding possibilities and delights that newness can bring."

—AIMEE MOISO,
associate director, Louisville Institute

Engaging the Gadfly

Engaging the Gadfly

Reflective Online, Hybrid, and In-Person Preaching in a Digital Age

CASEY T. SIGMON

Foreword by John S. McClure

CASCADE *Books* • Eugene, Oregon

ENGAGING THE GADFLY
Reflective Online, Hybrid, and In-Person Preaching in a Digital Age

Copyright © 2025 Casey T. Sigmon. All rights reserved. Except for brief quotations in critical publications or reviews, no part of this book may be reproduced in any manner without prior written permission from the publisher. Write: Permissions, Wipf and Stock Publishers, 199 W. 8th Ave., Suite 3, Eugene, OR 97401.

Cascade Books
An Imprint of Wipf and Stock Publishers
199 W. 8th Ave., Suite 3
Eugene, OR 97401

www.wipfandstock.com

PAPERBACK ISBN: 978-1-6667-7557-0
HARDCOVER ISBN: 978-1-6667-7558-7
EBOOK ISBN: 978-1-6667-7559-4

Cataloguing-in-Publication data:

Names: Sigmon, Casey T., author. | McClure, John S., foreword author.

Title: Engaging the gadfly : reflective online, hybrid, and in-person preaching in a digital age / Casey T. Sigmon; foreword by John S. McClure.

Description: Eugene, OR: Cascade Books, 2025 | Includes bibliographical references and index.

Identifiers: ISBN 978-1-6667-7557-0 (paperback) | ISBN 978-1-6667-7558-7 (hardcover) | ISBN 978-1-6667-7559-4 (ebook)

Subjects: LCSH: Preaching. | Communication—Religious aspects—Christianity. | Social media. | Cyberspace—Religious aspects.

Classification: BV4319 S45 2025 (paperback) | BV4319 (ebook)

VERSION NUMBER 06/05/25

Scripture quotations are taken from the New Revised Standard Version Updated Edition. Copyright © 2021 National Council of Churches of Christ in the United States of America. Used by permission. All rights reserved worldwide.

Scripture taken from *THE MESSAGE*. Copyright © 1993, 1994, 1995, 1996, 2000, 2001, 2002. Used by permission of NavPress Publishing Group.

Figure 4.1: The Objectivist Myth of Knowing and Figure 4.2: The Community of Truth. Used with permission of from John Wiley & Sons-Books, The Courage to Teach: Exploring the Inner Landscape of a Teacher's Life, Parker Palmer, 2007; permission conveyed through Copyright Clearance Center, Inc.

For #thatguyphill #ladyvisigburgh #lilflosigburgh

Contents

List of Illustrations and Tables | x

Foreword by John S. McClure | xi

Acknowledgments | xv

Introduction | xix

1   Why Bother Preaching? | 1

2   We've Seen This Shift Before: The Gadfly in Protestant Preaching Reformation(s) and Print Technoculture | 20

3   Communication Breakdown: Exploring the Pupal Stage of the Gadfly in the 1960s | 40

4   Oh, Shifts! Meeting the Gadfly of This Digital Age | 60

5   Preaching in the Age of Chatbots | 85

6   A New Media Homilecclesiology: Of Touch in the Digital Age | 98

7   Reflective Preaching Practice for a Digital Age | 125

Appendix | 153

Bibliography | 161

List of Illustrations and Tables

Figure 1 The Gadfly
Figure 2 The Papal Belvedere by Lucas Cranach, the Elder
Figure 3 Palmer, "Mythical Objectivism"
Figure 4 Palmer, "Community of Truth"
Table 1 Dialogue Compared to Debate

Foreword

JOHN S. MCCLURE

CHURCH LEADERS HAVE STRUGGLED to understand and effectively integrate emerging technologies for as long as the church has been in existence. The printing press, pipe organs, electric lights, sound systems, overhead projection, electric guitars and keyboards, and many other technologies have presented themselves, like so many pesky gadflies (as Professor Sigmon sees them) provoking us to avoid them, swat them to one side, or to learn what it is that they might want from us. If you prefer to avoid or shun emerging communication technologies, this is not the book for you. Dr. Sigmon is an optimist at heart. She believes that many of our most recent media technologies can, and should, be carefully and cautiously embraced.

The setting for this book is the post-pandemic church. Because of the pandemic, most churches suddenly found themselves thrust headlong into the communication technology game, whether they wanted to play or not. Worship services were recorded on smart phones or other devices and broadcast on Zoom, YouTube, and other platforms. Preachers found themselves preaching from their kitchens or living rooms, looking at camera lenses or small boxes of church members on computer screens. At the same time, choirs struggled to continue some form of music ministry in virtual spaces. Now that the pandemic has subsided, many questions linger. Should we continue to make use of these and other emerging communication technologies? What are the key issues that each new technology poses for preaching and worship? How do new media technologies challenge our understanding of church and theological categories such as incarnation and sacramental theology? Can we continue to worship without human bodies coming into proximity with one another physically? What does virtual reality add and/or subtract from physical reality? What new theological frameworks do we need to think more clearly about where God is amid this current technological revolution? What does this revolution require of us if we are to follow God faithfully today?

Beyond the communication technologies that suddenly swarmed the church like gadflies during the pandemic, Dr. Sigmon wants us to consider what implications artificial intelligence will have on ministry. For instance, how will sermon preparation change under the influence of AI? What aspects of human creativity are both enhanced and threatened by AI, and how can we think about God's creative action in our midst when artificial intelligence has become a new godlike creative force to contend with on a day-to-day basis?

Dr. Sigmon has spent the last ten years (at least) thinking deeply about these and other core questions that our new technologies pose for us. Although forward-thinking, and keenly interested in the integration of new media technologies into the life of the church, she is also very mindful that, like the humans that make them, these technologies are liable to brokenness and sinfulness. Rather than adopting either a naively optimistic or strictly post-human approach, she sees the all-too-human elements that are embedded within these technologies and raises key questions about them. These questions are very helpful for those of us who wish to think clearly about using new technologies on behalf of the churches we serve. At bottom, Professor Sigmon is looking for a theological approach that is not easily dated as technology advances. She helps us identify enduring theological ideas that we can see at work in the development and use of certain technologies; ideas that we can keep before us as we critique and make use of them.

Practically, this book is very helpful for those of us who want to know what these new technologies might require of us in the "big picture." Dr. Sigmon helps us investigate how we will need to rethink our views of authority, our own roles as leaders, among others, and the likely implications of certain technologies for the mundane practices we have come to cherish. In all things, Professor Sigmon will not let us sit still, with our fingers in our ears and our eyes closed, denying the real impact of these technological gadflies. She is convinced that they signal new possibilities for broader, multigenerational, and multimodal ways to communicate the gospel. She is a process theologian and a process thinker, for whom *becoming* and especially becoming in the image of God and toward God, is all-important.

Foreword

Elements from the past and the present need to morph and change as they encounter the divine possibilities that God is placing before us as new technologies come into view.

As I read this book, I found my mind changed several times, and my creativity challenged repeatedly by the insights and suggestions that Professor Sigmon very gently, and with good humor, nudged before me. I grew up on a farm, and we were not very fond of flies, especially horse flies. After reading this book, I have a new appreciation for a very different kind of flies, the creative gadflies of new technologies that promise enhanced communication, interaction, and learning in today's churches. I have now decided to lay down my curmudgeonly fly swatter and see what might happen if I allow myself to engage with some of these fascinating technological critters on behalf of the communication of the gospel. I am likely to get bitten a few times, but in the end, I expect to have a better-informed and wiser way of thinking and acting on behalf of the church-to-come.

Acknowledgments

It is no exaggeration to say this project could not exist without my incredible network of relationships. The first hub of connection I will mention is my homiletics family: Vanderbilt H&L Papas John S. McClure and the late, great, so very missed Dale P. Andrews. Thank you both for nurturing my engagement with the gadfly of technology for preaching in the first place. And thank you for cultivating a homiletics collective that I still turn to for encouragement, wisdom, empathy, and *fun*—gratitude to my #VandyHandL family. John, thank you for contributing a foreword to this text. I am so inspired by your decades of innovative research in homiletics.

Thank you, Aimee Moiso, my #VandyHandL sister. Aimee generously was my conversation partner and editor of the first drafts of this book. You don't know how much your guidance kept me going in the past year. You helped me claim my voice and break old imposter syndrome habits.

Thank you, Saint Paul student Joyce McCarty, for taking on the fun work of formatting a manuscript!

Thank you to the Academy of Homiletics, especially Karyn Wiseman, for creating a dialogical space for the "Preaching, Technology, and Media" scholarship to find a home in the guild. Rob O'Lynn, you've been a fantastic dialogue partner and book suggester! Jake Myers, thanks for connecting me with Matthew Wimer, Rodney Clapp, and the team at Cascade.

Saint Paul School of Theology has been my laboratory since 2016, when I taught my first elective on the topic of preaching in the digital age. Remember how proud we were, PRE 444 class, when that blizzard hit, and you all took to Facebook Live to create a worship space for your congregations? We felt like explorers! I will never forget those first students: Dan Norwood, Linda Jones, Jake Tatarian, Jay Wiesner, Dana Spears, Ginger

Acknowledgments

Rothhaas, Cassie Graham, Dennis Irwin, Curt Magelky, Tazoona Jacob Maforo, and Sangyeop Han. Thanks for bravely hosting TweetChat sermons, bracing through the terrible emoji Bible exercise, and refining my theories and methods with curiosity, enthusiasm, and generosity.

And thank you, former Saint Paul student Abby Peper, for serving as a research assistant and conversation partner as I brought the dissertation into a form more suitable to a broad public. Your connection of Phyllis Tickle to Priya Parker was inspiring! Not as inspiring as the ways you embody a new media homilecclesiology at the Table. And that cartoon of the Gadfly you gifted me that I now keep on my office door.

Before COVID, I met two other colleagues at Saint Paul with as much excitement about technology and theology as I had: Samantha Potter and Nancy Howell. We formed TheoTechnics together. Our collaboration, workshops, and discussions are a thread throughout this book. And special thanks to The Bridge for Early Career Preachers at Union Presbyterian Seminary, led by my friend and #VandyHandL brother Rich Voelz and Mandy Cole, for inviting us to share our work with early career preachers in your Lilly Compelling Preaching program.

I had a chance to share this research with Myers Park Baptist Church in Charlotte, North Carolina, in October 2023. Thank you, Ben Boswell and Tara Gibbs, for inviting me to keynote your Faith in the 21st Century event on "Church of the Future: Faith in a Network Age."

Although I am ordained in the Christian Church (Disciples of Christ), my position at a United Methodist seminary has connected me to their global network. I am especially grateful to Laura Murphy at the Missouri United Methodist Foundation for seeing the need for UMC pastors to receive coaching on digital discipleship. Thank you, Trista Soendker Nicholson, for inviting me to teach the February 2023 Missouri UMC Preaching Academy on preaching in the digital age. Those workshops also helped shape this book and motivate me through the long writing process. I hope this book will inspire conversations in even more congregations like the ones we shared and continue to share.

Thanks to the Ugly Club for daily inspiration and pep. I love you all forever.

And, of course, my family. The hub and heart of my life. Thank you. Thank you, Phill, for being with me through the days of writing when I didn't believe I had a thing to add to the conversation. You bring out the best in me and our daughters every day. Thank you, Viola and Lillian, for

Acknowledgments

your patience and nudging me into impromptu dance parties that kept me sane (especially during the pandemic home school year). I hope this little contribution helps create a healthier, more caring, effective, vulnerable, and prophetic church for you. I hope it helps you navigate this digital age without wavering in your love for God, your neighbors, and yourself.

Gratitude is the name of the game. It's part of what makes us and keeps us human in the digital age. That extends to you, dear human. Thank you for engaging the Gadfly with me. This work is for you and your faith community.

Casey Thornburgh Sigmon
On the thirteenth anniversary of my ordination in the Christian Church (Disciples of Christ)
June 12, 2024

Introduction

Christianity is a community possessed, according to the Christian faith, with a unique vitality that stems from its animation by the Spirit of the risen Christ. For this reason, the faith and experience and life forms of the New Testament communities, uniquely normative though they may be for future generations, can never be the static pattern for those future generations. As an eschatological reality the church is always coming into being, always new in a radical and sometimes unexpected fashion.[1]

—Bernard J. Cooke

MAKING DO

Well, now we've done it.

For the most part anyway, I think it's safe to say we've all done it:

Preached online. Or preached to a laptop in an empty room. Or preached from a pulpit to an empty sanctuary. Or picked up the phone to preach live from a platform.

Pat yourselves on the back, preachers. You've done it. With creativity that you found hidden within, just when you thought you didn't have an ounce more to give to ministry in a pandemic.

This book is for you.

And congratulations, congregants, because you've done it.

1. Cooke, *Ministry to Word and Sacraments*, 58.

Introduction

Streamed online worship. Fumbled with meeting IDs and passwords. Watched an online sermon and posted in the chat or adding hearts, thumbs up, or smiley faces to a Live sermon.

This book is also for you.

Because now you may be wondering together about next steps.

Some might be pushing for a step back into the ways of local preaching and worship before March 2020.

This book is for you.

Some might be eager to be back in the sanctuary, but also curious about how best to move forward without losing a faithful part of the congregation for whom online services have been a godsend after years of being apart, due to any number of conditions.

This book is for you.

Some congregations were born out of the pandemic, gathered online from all parts of the country, even world. As other churches return to normal, these churches are living into a new normal and wondering how to gather around the word of God well. What are our norms? Values? How do we do this new thing with integrity?

This book is also for you.

All certainly experienced (or are still experiencing) change fatigue. Slipping back into familiar ways of preaching and leading worship feels like a warm blanket on a blustery evening, a cool drink of water on a scorching afternoon.

Because let's face it. We are tired of "making do."

COVID-19 AND THE SEASON OF MAKING DO

It is helpful to reframe our attempts preaching online during the pandemic as artful means of "making do" with what we had, finding freedom and agency to preach and worship within the confines of COVID protocols and media platforms.

I play with the concept of "making do" from French Jesuit sociologist Michel de Certeau's term *bricolage*.[2] *Bricolage* is a French word that translates into English as "fiddling" or "tinkering." What does tinkering have to do with preaching in a digital age? De Certeau is not specifically speaking to a post-pandemic church when he describes the sociological phenomenon of making do. A contemporary phrase for what he describes could be

---

2. De Certeau, *Practice*, 29.

INTRODUCTION

"coping strategies." Specifically, in *The Practice of Everyday Life*, he observes the ways people produce and use or engage culture. Ordinary people do not have the power to produce the megastructures we culturally inhabit. The elite or ruling class do. According to de Certeau, ordinary people have been marginalized in our current consumer culture. Nonetheless, ordinary people within the cultural structures put in place by the elite/ruling class can and do find ways of making do and subversively producing new meaning unintended by the producers within the system. This may be done by individuals (engaging what de Certeau calls "tactics") and by institutions (engaging what de Certeau calls "strategies"). You will likely notice this book dancing between both as we reflect on hearing, creating, and sharing sermons in this digital age.

Let me put it another way. We do not have complete control over the world created by and through media. We will talk more about this in the chapters ahead. However, we have response-ability, that is some wiggle room to make do within the context we find ourselves in and to hold space for our interests, mission, purpose, and imagination.

When we were forced to worship and preach online, we were invited (a gentler phrase than forced) to make do and make a place for meaningful assembly in virtual spaces. Schools, family systems, and churches created for themselves "a space in which" they "can find *ways of using* the constraining order" without abandoning "the place where" they may have "no choice but to live."[3]

For months, preachers and congregants had no choice but to live out our vocation within the confines of masks, social distance, building capacity limits, broadband limits, etc. And in the midst of making do, preachers and congregants discovered some new ways of being the church that did not fit in the former patterns. As the sermon was live-streamed, we discovered that we could talk during the sermon (in a chat room, comments section, or in our homes) and not be shushed for inserting our voices into the sermonic moment. We discovered that we did not have to worry so much about our children's need to physically move around during worship because there weren't neighbors in our pew trying to focus on the sermon. We discovered the new insights that come to the preacher's mind when they move from the pulpit to the kitchen table.

---

3. De Certeau, *Practice*, 30. Emphasis his.

Introduction

Perhaps we discovered in the making do that some of the frames that felt confining during COVID restrictions also revealed a constraining order to our ordinary worship that we had not felt before.

Many aspects of technology indeed need to be subverted rather than humbly accepted as reality. The internet or Metaverse are not utopias where the church can finally be the real church! The polarization amplified by algorithms and the broken ways of speaking with and listening to each other should not be accepted by the church as the way things are. However, online and in person within this digital culture we now inhabit are tactics for subversion and prophetic creativity. And this book will suggest some of them as it invites congregations to see engagement in our digital age with more than a "making do" attitude.

Beautiful ministries were born and are being born of this season. Can they fit into the order of worship as it ordinarily exists? What's changing in the ways we gather for worship, and why?

THE GADFLY

Change is not always a welcome guest in the halls of institutional life. Often, it looms large like an elephant in the room of our organizations and denominations. Or perhaps it is more appropriate to say that the buzzing of change in the halls of institutional life is more like the buzz of the Gadfly—more difficult to grasp, quick to dodge the hand or tail that swat at it, and just when you think the one has died, another Gadfly just as annoying appears in its place.

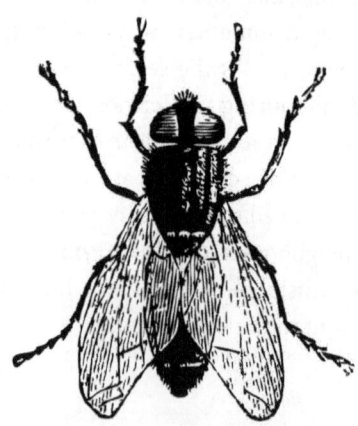

Introduction

Process philosopher and mathematician Alfred North Whitehead used the image of the Gadfly to describe the presence of new ideas, novelty, in the face of institutional structures. He chose the Gadfly, or common housefly, because new ideas are always a nuisance that seems small, yet in time their buzzing is "a danger to the existing order."[4] The last thirty years of evolution from dial-up internet (cue the sound of a modem for readers aged elder millennial—cough, cough, me—and older) to smartphones and now ChatGPT. Buzz . . . buzz. So many challenges to existing structures. Including the church. Including the practice of preaching.

It's safe to say that I am pretty much a suburban/urban dweller. I like the buzz of community that proximity to neighbors offers. I like coffee shop choices rather than a single option on Main Street. I like public transit, getting lost in a new block, being one of many in the zip code. I also prefer suburban/urban flies to country flies.

Have you encountered a country fly? I mean, let's be honest, they hardly resemble a fly. They make noise like a passing jet. You can see them out of the corner of your eye before they land and bite, *bite*, your flesh. My aunt and uncle lived in a rural area outside of Topeka, Kansas. In the summer, my suburbanite self and my sisters would spend a week with our rural cousins. Most of that time, Aunt Linda sent us outside to explore, create worlds, and watch storms bloom over the horizon. Then, once a day, we would get to ride horses.

Horses are amazing creatures. But their presence also invites an unwelcome creature known as the horsefly. And those monsters sure can bite. Lured by the aroma of the horse's excreta, you can bet that a horsefly is never far from a horse (especially in Kansas). Not only is feces a delightful scent to flies (picture a fly in its home lighting a Yankee candle called "Essence of Dung" here), flies make a meal of the bacteria found in animal waste.

> *Whoa, whoa, whoa, Casey. What on earth is this book about? I thought we were going to talk about preaching online!*

Stay with me . . . I am painting a picture (it's what we preachers do for a living). We are, after all, about to meet the Gadfly that is hovering around the church and society in the midst of these unprecedented shifts. I don't mean to be crass here, but rest assured: the presence of big shifts in culture invites the presence of Gadflies.

---

4. Whitehead, *Adventures*, 15.

Introduction

See what I did there?

Where there is *shift*, there is *Gadfly*—buzzing around as the shift fertilizes new ideas, new structures, and new ways of being.

The context and framework for preaching, as it existed for centuries in the Western church, is the pulpit to the pew. This structure assumes that preaching occurs in a sanctuary, which logically means the event occurs within the architecture of a house of worship designed in such a way to best host the communication of the spoken word to a group of listeners in the pews below.

Now, in the haze of technological change, a Gadfly appears. In the words of Whitehead, its ideas and invitations for preaching and the church are "at once gadflies irritating, and beacons luring, the victims among whom they dwell."[5] I prefer the notion that the new ideas are not intended to threaten the existing order in totality by doing away with *all* preaching as it exists in most of our churches on Sunday morning. Yet, I do think these new ideas, and habits born of making do during COVID, are Gadflies, beacons luring the field of homiletics and the practice of preaching to innovative, creative, and prophetic embodiments ripe for this day and age.

Here are some examples of what I mean about the Gadfly's buzz in the forms of questions I've heard preachers and congregants raise out of March 2020: Maybe listeners can talk during the sermon? Maybe sermons are too wordy? Maybe one person telling the story of God for us is not the only way to hear God speaking? Is recording and posting sermons on YouTube an adequate way to reach people online? This buzz results from the Gadflies of technological and technocultural change. COVID-19 only sped up what I believe was an inevitable shift from a dominant print technoculture to social media and digital technoculture. Will we stop to engage the Gadfly together? Or swat it away to grasp at preaching as usual?

This book is an enduring conversation with—rather than swatting at or ignoring—the Gadfly of our digital age. This book invites weary preachers and congregants to join the conversation together. Ultimately, this digital age, like previous ages of technological change, presents problems as well as possibilities, to the practice of preaching, and so, ecclesiology—the shape of the church. We will explore both in the chat with the Gadfly ahead.

---

5. Whitehead, *Adventures*, 18.

Introduction

SHOO, FLY! DON'T BOTHER ME

In the late winter of 2022, as the Omicron variant of COVID-19 appeared to be on its way out and churches once again saw an opportunity to regather in buildings, an op-ed was published in *The New York Times* that boldly argued "Why Churches Should Drop Their Online Services."[6] According to the author, online worship "diminishes worship and us as people. We seek to worship wholly—with heart, soul, mind and strength—and embodiment is an irreducible part of that wholeness."[7]

This book will help you complexify the assumptions embedded within this line of thinking, assumptions such as we aren't using our bodies when we join a Zoom call, make a FaceTime, or enter the Metaverse. Then, on the flipside is the assumption that we do a good job of leading and participating in embodied liturgy when we are in person. As if, simply by virtue of being in the same room together, we are worshiping wholly.[8] The tone I pick up in this op-ed is basically: Shoo, fly! Don't bother me . . .

Counterarguments spread through the internet immediately. Most of the arguments challenged the author for writing from a place of physical privilege, including this one from Shannon Dingle in her essay, "Quitting Online Church is Abandoning the One for the 99."

> Consider, for a moment, that the story is one disabled person and 99 abled people, and instead of a field, the setting is a church. When one needed to be able to participate in the community of believers from home or a hospital using technology, we in the church stuck with the 99. Those virtual church options that were called impossible for the one became possible when COVID-19 safety measures, like not meeting in person, were necessary for the remaining 99 as well. The accommodation was never impossible for the one. We made a choice that the 99 abled people were worthy of such an option becoming available, which revealed what we believed about the one disabled person: They alone were not worthy, not in how church worked prior to the pandemic.[9]

The Gadfly revealed what many on the margins already knew: traditional ways of preaching and worshiping privileged abled bodies. Additionally,

---

6. Warren, "Why Churches Should Drop Their Online Services."
7. Warren, "Why Churches Should Drop Their Online Services."
8. I challenged this assumption in another article: Sigmon, "Failure to Discern the Online Body/Hybrid Body."
9. Dingle, "Quitting Online Church is Abandoning the One for the 99."

Introduction

as folks sought and found welcoming worshiping communities online that were not within driving distance, the mainstream saw how preaching and worship in the traditional sense favor straight, monogamous, cisgender preachers and congregants. Decades before March 2020, queer, chronically ill, deconstructing Christians were assembling online, through platforms like Second Life, to create beloved communities when conventional worship houses prevented them from worshiping wholly—mind, body, and soul. Preaching occurred online, in simulated worlds, and on social media platforms, before March 2020. But the church and academy did not take much notice of it before.

THE LAY OF THE LAND

This book is organized in two parts. The first (chapters 1 through 5) helps both pastor and congregation discern the lay of the land in our digital age through historical connections. Part two (chapters 6 and 7) offers a theological approach to and practices for reflective preaching in this digital age. Throughout this book, I will address the pastor and community with the expectation that this book will be a *shared dialogue.*

Chapter 1 asks the reader to explore their answer to the question: *why even bother preaching in the digital age?* Preaching practices should always begin with the *why* or purpose. It also explains a theology of incarnation to help frame our engagement with the Gadfly. You will also meet the term *homilecclesiology* and hear me explain why I think it is an apt term for the study and practice of preaching in the digital age.

Chapter 2 will also offer some historical examples of how preaching responded to shifts in technoculture in the past. You also will get a definition of technoculture! Some wise person once said there is nothing new under the sun (oh hey, it's Scripture!). Exploring how our forebears adapted may give us collective courage to do likewise in our time and place. We've seen this shift before.

Chapter 3 explores how homileticians and pastoral theologians in the twentieth century began to engage the buzz of the Gadfly as they questioned the formational impact of broadcast preaching on the church. These thinkers will question the efficacy of monological preaching and push the reader to see the value of congregational participation in preaching.

Chapter 4 brings us to the rapid cultural and technological shifts of the last thirty years. We will learn a framework for engaging these changes

Introduction

with discernment instead of swatting them away as irrelevant or harmful or grasping at technological change as the savior of the world. One of the critical shifts born of our present technoculture is more participatory communication. Chapter 5 is a short exploration into generative artificial intelligence and why it matters to preaching. This discussion includes what it means to be human in the age of AI and chatbots.

Chapter 6 describes a new media homilecclesiology that engages, instead of ignores, the Gadfly of this digital age. The fundamentals of this homiletic method, informed by tradition and the realities of this digital age, will help us transition into digital-dialogical practice.

Chapter 7 takes this homiletic into play. We explore digital-dialogical practices for the analog church, sermon preparation, and delivery. The strategies can be adapted to conventional monological sermons and for communities that want to bring dialogue into the sermon event. An appendix at the back of the book helps the reader(s) set goals for implementing the lessons of this book in their time and place.

MY JOURNEY IN ENGAGING THE GADFLY

When I started this adventure in academia in 2011, I did not see myself as becoming a "technology" expert in homiletics. I had other ideas in mind. But during my time in graduate studies at Vanderbilt, something (so many things, really) changed.

In 2017, fresh from defending my dissertation, I brought my research on preaching in the digital age into the Saint Paul School of Theology classroom. My students dabbled in Tweet chat sermons, Facebook Live sermons, and Instagram story sermon snippets in that space. We had fun. When a snowstorm blew through Kansas that winter, students jumped at the chance to apply their practices directly to their ministry settings and hosted some of their first worship services online. We never knew how grateful we'd be for these experiences just a few years later.

Never in my wildest dreams did I imagine a pandemic that would thrust the whole world into "making do" with online forms of preaching. I figured I'd remain an oddball homiletician talking about social media, avatars, and AI for the decades I'd be teaching. I was wrong!

Now, you've been immersed in various technologies to lead and participate in worship. And now, as you discern as a congregation what the new normal is in this technological landscape, we have new and hard-earned

INTRODUCTION

insights, experiences, and questions to bring to all of worship and the work of discipleship, including preaching.

As we will discuss later, sociologists and historians argue that we are now on the brink of a shift in communication as transformative as the invention of the printing press. No wonder ministry is so challenging right now. Through this book, I invite the preacher/pastor to gather with their congregation to process these shifts and consider how they are being invited to engage the Gadfly of technological change for preaching in their time and place.

In this social media world, how now shall we preach? In the age of generative artificial intelligence, how now shall we preach? Let's explore together.

CONVERSATION PROMPTS:

1. How did you and your congregation "make do" during COVID?
2. Did you engage in digital ministry prior to March 2020? How?
3. Have you kept any digital practices alive since returning to in-person worship? Why or why not?

1

Why Bother Preaching?

"Of course, church has theological definitions, such as 'the Body of Christ,' the community of the redeemed, the locus where the sacraments are celebrated, the place where Christians gather for worship, teaching, and community. But what church actually is has always been deeply affected by the world around it. When that world changes, so too does church. Everyone acknowledges that we are living in a time of revolutionary change. So tell me why we don't think church is in for some radical changes?"

—Philip Clayton

"Christianity itself is a mediated phenomenon, one in which the matrix of mediation within which it takes shape at any particular period of history is integral to its character."

—Peter Horsfield

Why do we even bother to preach?

Maybe you didn't expect a preaching book to start with this question. *I thought this book was on preaching and technology! Talk about false advertising . . .*

Clearly, I see value in preaching. Otherwise, why write a book about it? But we start with asking "why do we even bother to preach?" because asking why we do something can remind us why this element of most worship services is worth passing on to future generations of Christians.

So, to ask the question differently, in a world of so much noise, why do *preaching* words matter?

Because, let's be honest, it's a wordy world. When I type out a sermon manuscript, I average two to three thousand words. This equates to roughly twenty to twenty-five minutes with my pace (and the occasional journey I take away from the script into images and ideas that come to me in the preaching event). Preachers, if you preach fifty-two sermons each year within my average word count (which is pretty low compared to folks who preach for forty minutes or more), you write 104,000–156,000 words typed and spoken each year. And the person listening to every sermon hears 1,040–1,300 minutes of preaching each year.

Most of us who preach and come to hear preaching on a Sunday accept the normal shape of the practice without asking why it came to be or why it still is. We write a sermon to fill twenty minutes. It will have touchpoints with Scripture, stories, and implied or direct implications for listeners. In the pew, we expect the preacher to say something about Scripture, teach us about Jesus, God, and the Holy Spirit, and leave us with some new idea, feeling, or action to implement after hearing the sermon.

While not all communities or traditions that identify themselves as Christian consistently incorporate sermons into their public worship, most do. This is an enduring practice in our tradition(s). We have evidence of sermons going back centuries. In the late fourth century, when the preservation of spoken words was costly and rare and required tedious recording by hand, the impactful and practical sermons of John Chrysostom ("The Golden Mouthed") were preserved for future generations of Christians.

We also get glimpses of preaching practices in the Scriptures: Jesus preaches in the synagogue a blissfully short yet powerful sermon (Luke 4); women and men who encounter the power of Jesus go home to tell/testify/preach the good news, such as a man blind from birth who was healed when Jesus made mud out of his spit and dirt and spread it on his eyes (John 9:1–7), or the Samaritan woman at a well who testifies in her hometown, "He told me everything I have ever done," and many believed (John 4:39). The writer of Acts describes multiple instances of apostolic preaching, especially examples of going outside of the inner circle, such as Peter preaching in Cornelius's house (Acts 10) and then later preaching to his inner circle about the need to welcome gentiles who received the Holy Spirit (Acts 11).

Why preach? Because it's something Christians—those who have encountered and experienced the healing power of Jesus—have done for a long time to express and encourage the body of Christ, bring people to Jesus, remind them of their identity, and correct behavior or dangerous beliefs when necessary.

However, doing something because "we've always done it that way" is not a particularly strong foundation. If the habit becomes the justification, we become disconnected from deeper theological and formational reasons for the practice. When we fall into habits, we can forget why a community established their practices in the first place.

Jesus preached in the synagogue because the holy words of the Torah—read, heard, and interpreted—contained meaning and direction for God's people in every time and place. Jesus' community heard his interpretation and reacted strongly to it. Apostles preached in Acts because they'd been empowered by the Holy Spirit and sent (the root meaning of the word "apostle") to spread the good news of Jesus the Messiah, who rose from the dead and defeated the efforts of the Roman Empire to silence the Way. People in the Gospels who encountered a miracle, healing, or the forgiveness of Jesus went home to share their stories, hoping it would bring others to Jesus for similar transformation.

Two thousand years later, I ask: Why do you preach on Sunday? And why do you come to church to listen to a sermon?

In a world where we can pull out our phones and text with Jesus (a real app, by the way, *TextsWithJesus*—and you can text Mary and Joseph, too) or play sermons from YouTube on demand, why come to worship on Sunday for a live, synchronous sermon event?

In a world with so many words already, why even bother with preaching? Why write, speak, and listen to more words? Can preaching words cut through the blizzard of other words in our world (including worship) to impact our lives? Our world?

The Gadfly you met in the Introduction is a metaphor for the pestering hum of change that hovers around institutions on the precipice of death and/or resurrection. That same Gadfly buzzes incessantly around the question of *why*, surfacing the question from deep within institutions in transition, including the institution of Christian worship.

You probably picked up this book because you've heard buzzing and are now asking as a congregation, how do we effectively preach in a digital age? In order to get to a more compelling *how*, I am going to invite you to start with *why*. By the end of this book, you will be able to articulate your reasons more clearly. Additionally, you will be able to evaluate how the way you preach or frame the sermon event aligns with the *why*.

Unfortunately, many workshops, podcasts, and blogs bombard pastors and congregations with *how* without holding space for *why*. Let's take a look at why this is problematic.

THE GADFLY & WHY?

If I had a dollar for every time someone mentioned Priya Parker's *The Art of Gathering* to me in the past few years, I'd be able to buy myself a five-course meal in one of Kansas City's many hip, award-winning restaurants. (The hype is real! I'm pretty sure I've suggested the book to just as many people, if not more than a five-course meal's worth.)

The heart of Parker's book is the claim that the *how* of any gathering should always be in touch with the *why* behind it. Our calendars are full of meetings and gatherings. Parker argues that we spend so many days in meetings that they have lost meaning. The Gadfly certainly makes its presence known to us in many of these meetings, leading us to wonder, *Couldn't this have been an email? Did we accomplish anything? This was a waste of time.*

As a result, we aren't reaping the full benefits that meetings and gatherings offer, such as transformation and connection among the people in these meetings with us. Parker laments that we don't make the most of precious gathering time because "we spend much of that time in uninspiring, underwhelming moments that fail to capture us, change us in any way, or connect us to one another."[1]

The category of "meetings" is not limited to work or committees. Worship services on Sunday are a meeting of people assembling to give thanks to God and grow as disciples of Christ. When established by a particular community at a particular time, meetings are strongly linked to a specific purpose. But as they become a habit, routine, or, as Parker says, "ritualized gatherings," the form—not just the purpose—of these meetings play "a

---

1. Parker, *Gathering*, ix–x.

role in shaping people's sense of belonging to the group and their identity within that group," with or without a sense of the purpose.[2] She illustrates:

> A specific gavel is always used. A certain turtleneck is always worn. People come to expect these elements of form and even take comfort in them.[3]

When the leader first used the gavel, was it meant to be an enduring practice or was it simply available and a means to cut through the conversation and call the meeting to order? When a CEO wore a particular turtleneck, was she planning to wear the item forever or was it what was clean and available in her closet that morning?

These may seem inconsequential until we turn this sort of questioning toward our most regular meetings in church life, including worship gatherings. *Why do we have a children's moment? Why do we print and fold bulletins when everything is on the screen?*

Or . . .

Why don't we just go back to the way we worshiped before March 2020 and stop engaging in online/hybrid endeavors?

When I read *The Art of Gathering* for the first time, I was teaching an independent study with a student who wanted to write and research fresh expressions of Christian worship. The student integrated Parker in her essay and Phyllis Tickle's *The Great Emergence*, suggesting that these new expressions of worship result from the sort of critical reflection that happens cyclically in the Latinized church. Tickle's 2012 book clarified a possible reason for the emerging ecclesiology shifts gaining momentum in the early twenty-first century. She used a historical framing to illustrate that about every five hundred years, Christians hold a "rummage sale" of accumulated habits, artifacts, and the meanings attached to them, and some new forms of church emerge. Briefly, these shifts took place around the years 500 (the fall of Rome), 1000 (schism between the church in the East and West), and 1500 (reformations, including the Protestant Reformation). *The Great Emergence* claimed that the historical moment of critique and creativity the church was feeling in 2012 was the beginning of a new rummage sale that anticipated the emergence of new forms. Five hundred years after Luther's Nintey-Five Theses were nailed to a door in Wittenberg, church leaders in

---

2. Parker, *Gathering*, 11.
3. Parker, *Gathering*, 11.

this era will again call out forms and meanings that need reconsideration, removal, and renovation (oh hey, are we talking about a reformation?).

Brilliantly, my student placed Tickle and Parker in conversation. She described how her church took advantage of the disruption of COVID to ask: Why do we gather for worship in the first place, and is the way that we worship helping us accomplish that why? In other words, my student asked: if our *why* for meeting is to build a beloved community of service and worship where God knows us as we know and love our neighbor, is a passive form in which we sit still on a pew and watch worship done by a few people up front going to help us reach the aim? In my student's view, not at all. She decided that it wasn't. A reconstruction of the *why* in her own church energized the changes. Even though the church had recently invested in a new stage to support better worship performance on stage, they were convicted by the invitation to reconsider the efficacy of spectator worship for building up a community. Pews were replaced with round tables. Setting up for worship involved hosting neighbors needing food assistance through a pantry set up like a grocery store, honoring their dignity. And the worship service became a dinner church. The sermon became a shared proclamation around tables, and communion was woven into the meal and sermon dialogue. Now, she has a flourishing dinner church that serves as a hub for fellowship and support in an underserved part of Kansas City.

The Gadfly is hovering over the forms of worship today and asking us with its incessant buzz, "Why?" *Why meet in a sanctuary built for 500 when fifty turn up on a good Sunday? Why continue to livestream worship if most of us are back in the building? Why learn new, modern worship songs when we have plenty of hymns in the hymnal? Why are four Main Street churches holding worship at the same time with only a handful of folks in each location?*

In this book, we are not just asking about the "whys" of worship. Specifically, we are focused on the Gadfly's buzz about the sermon. *Why do we gather around a pulpit on Sunday mornings? Why do we expect a twenty- to forty-five-minute monologue from the pastor every week? Why has the practice of preaching persisted through previous rummage sales? And will it make it through this 500-year moment unchanged?*

Unchanged? Unlikely. In the biblical depictions of preaching at the beginning of this chapter, we see only one "pulpit" example, if any (Jesus in the synagogue may have used some platform to speak, but the *why* behind it was to be heard better—an example of technology before microphones). Preaching has not always and only been practiced by ordained church authority nor exclusively conducted in the setting of a worship service. Nonetheless, most of us only preach or hear sermons on Sunday in the context of a worship service, so we might assume that pulpits and pews are defining elements of a sermon and swat away anything buzzing around us that challenges these assumptions. As Parker cautioned, we might mistake the forms as essential to the ritualized gathering when in fact, they are not and may no longer be the best ways to accomplish the *why* behind our gathering.

WHY WE PREACH: INCARNATION

Okay. So, back to the opening question: why do we preach? Why do we gather to hear sermons?

I will offer a proposal for this *why* based on a theology of the incarnation. Reclaiming the good news revealed through incarnation is more important than ever. We live in an age where some find comfort and hope in a future that supersedes the flesh through technologies that can outperform and outlast our fleshy fragility. As artificial intelligence (AI) becomes easily accessible to the public—generating sermons or responding to text messages *as* Jesus,[4] for example—the need for "inefficient" human beings to do *anything* is being challenged. Would it be easier to ask a generative AI application like ChatGPT to write a sermon for every Sunday? Yes. But should we do that instead of paying a pastor to put their blood, sweat, and tears into crafting a sermon?

Buzz. Buzz. I hear the Gadfly.

Here is my reply: There is something essential to the human element of preaching and proclamation that cannot be discarded in this current rummage sale.

Let me explain through some human testimony.

I did not grow up in a Christian household. Our religion was pop culture and music, arts, and comedy filled our home. (*Remember 1980s MTV?*) We were "Catholic," but the sort of Catholic that went to Mass on Easter and Christmas and not much else. In high school, I was introduced to Christianity through a para-church organization whose method for sharing the gospel was relational, or what I would later learn to be "incarnational." An

---

4. See the app "TextsWithJesus." This app also lets you text Mary and Joseph for free! Other biblical figures? That will cost you.

early sermon that stuck with me was based on the prologue of the Gospel of John. I still remember the awe when I first heard:

> [1-2] The Word was first,
> the Word present to God,
> God present to the Word.
> The Word was God,
> in readiness for God from day one.
> [3-5] Everything was created through him;
> nothing—not one thing!—
> came into being without him.
> What came into existence was Life,
> and the Life was Light to live by.
> The Life-Light blazed out of the darkness;
> the darkness couldn't put it out.
>
> [14] The Word became flesh and blood,
> and moved into the neighborhood.[5]

Twenty-five years later, I remember not only the text but the sermon from the preacher that day as he described the glory of God—galactic, celestial, microscopic, infinite—choosing to dwell with us on our fleshy terms, starting as cells clustering within a young girl named Mary, and growing slowly into an adult who could articulate the love of God *with* us in ways trees, rocks, stones, and prophets alone could not.

The preacher used an example of a human-sized God trying to convey their love to a colony of ants, bending over and shouting, "*Hey! Ants! You are loved! Did you know that? I love you!*" Terrifying, right? So instead, the Creator of ants and all things chose to become an ant, from beginning to end, to incarnate the message.

Incarnation is essential to the messaging of the good news. God chose the inefficient, delicate medium of being human to convey God's Word to us. That is why humans preach and gather to hear preaching from other humans.

For centuries, human beings have leaned into this invitation to continue to share the message of Jesus, imperfectly and wonderfully. Through three previous ecclesial rummage sales, the incarnational messaging of the incarnation as Word and word of God through incarnation has persisted. And I do believe that it will persist through this epochal change.

---

5. John 1: 1–5; 14, *The Message*.

Why Bother Preaching?

The *why* for preaching is that it is an enduring incarnational activity that keeps humans in touch with the God who remains in touch with us. Like our ancestors before us, when we experience the healing touch of Jesus, we want to share it; we must share it. When we see a gap between the reality Jesus and the prophets proclaimed and the one we live in, we must preach about it. A preacher is anyone compelled and called to communicate some message of God's good news as it arises within her, out of a wrestling match with context and Word. In a worship service or beyond it, preaching endures when we have been touched and transformed by good news.

Moreover, God desires to shape our very embodiment of kin-dom values. The ongoing ministry activity of preaching good news *shapes the preacher*. The people who continually hear and interact with her as one shaped by this embodiment with the Word are also shaped distinctively. Preaching is incarnational because, like Jesus, it is an activity that is fully human and somehow divine by the Holy Spirit and through the living Word.

In this way, preaching is always related to ecclesiology. Ecclesiology is a theological word used to describe the study of the church—its shape, who leads it, and how it interacts with the world, local and global. For most of us, preaching takes place in "church." While there have been exceptions to this rule, preaching most often occurs from a pulpit in a church building in front of a congregation seated in pews. Preaching, though, does not exist for its own sake. Preaching is entangled with ecclesiology because preaching occurs within and for the sake of the church's ongoing spiritual and ethical formation. But neither does the church exist for its own sake! Preaching is not meant to only fortify the institution of church into an unchanging entity that endures unchanged by the shifts taking place "in the world." The church, shaped by preaching, engages and interacts with the world.

In English, the word *church* can be a noun and adjective. It can refer to a building, a worship service, or the clergy of a religious body. Church etymologically is the old English word used to translate the Greek word *ekklesia*, from which we get the word ecclesiology. *Ekklesia* is not associated with buildings or denominations. It means assembly or gathering of people who are called out in order to meet with a particular purpose. Location is not essential to the definition of *ekklesia*. Where individuals gather or congregate, there is a congregation.

I think it's safe to assume that most of us hear the word "church" and picture a building.

Engaging the Gadfly

Here's the church, here's the steeple, open the doors, and see all the people.

Before COVID-19, the four walls of the church building were often understood as a basic requirement for orthodox worship. The building itself was essential for efficient and effective sacramental and homiletical delivery. Economic well-being that allowed for denominations to construct houses of worship on the main streets of America (where the term "mainline" originates) contributed to an assumption that church is a place that we go for worship, and that Christians are people who follow Jesus by going to a building each Sunday to hear a sermon based on holy Scriptures and take communion weekly, quarterly, or anything in between.

Suppose we remove buildings, walls, pulpits, and pews from the picture of what constitutes a church and what defines preaching. What if "church" really did mean "assembly or gathering of people who are called out in order to meet with a particular purpose"? Could we consider the Gadfly of this digital age with more imagination?

It is difficult to imagine how to help preachers to be ready for that change. Our current systems and structures that teach preaching are set up to perpetuate the expectation of trained clergy speaking from a pulpit in a building to the laity in the pews. It is far easier to continue to plan and organize preaching as weekly speaking commitments in the context of worship, with perhaps funerals and weddings on occasion. As Marjorie Suchocki described in *The Whispered Word*, "Our structures, no matter how inclusive their original intent, tend to harden toward their own preservation and perpetuation, rather than to be continuously open to the needs of inclusive well-being."[6]

While this familiar form of preaching is indeed important and likely will not disappear on the other end of the rummage sale in this five-hundred-year moment, we also need the flexibility of emerging *hows* of preaching and church in order to be fluent with (respond to?) changing times. Whitehead, the one who introduced us to the Gadfly in the Introduction, names this paradox when he says,

> The paradox which wrecks so many promising theories of education is that the training which produces skill is so very apt to stifle imaginative zest. Skill demands repetition, and imaginative zest is tinged with impulse.[7]

---

6. Suchocki, *Whispered*, 141.
7. Whitehead, *Process and Reality*, 338.

WHY BOTHER PREACHING?

As we shift into conversations about virtual, online, and hybrid church, it will help us be imaginative and flexible to return to this early definition of church, ecclesiology, and *ekklesia*—not a denomination or physical building, but the act of people gathering. We can question the forms of this gathering (in a building, open field, on Zoom, etc.), but maybe the gathering does not require a specific building for the preaching event to occur and shape us. More on that later! Buzz. Buzz.

A VERY BRIEF INTRODUCTION TO PROCESS THEOLOGY

I have mentioned Alfred North Whitehead earlier in the book and will continue to do so throughout. He inspired my Gadfly metaphor, and his contributions to process theology are foundational to my perspective of who God is and how to respond faithfully to the one in whose image we are made (Gen 1).

Mention process theology and you may get contorted expressions and eye rolls that reveal the challenge of reading—let alone *processing*—Whitehead's work. Whitehead birthed the "process" movement in theological and philosophical thinking. He wrote primarily as a mathematician, not a theologian, yet his system and metaphors for conceiving reality resisted boundaries between hard and soft sciences and pursued holistic knowing. His concluding pages of *Process and Reality* ruminate on the relationship of God with the world as a window into the realities observed in geometry, measurement, and even consciousness. God, according to Whitehead, is in touch with all things in this world and beyond, and we are able and encouraged to remain in touch with this God who is omnipresent (always present).

Tragically, according to Whitehead, Christianity has engaged philosophical worldviews that contrast with an omnipresent God. He specifically challenges the Aristotelian influence that casts God as a distant "un-moved mover" who is over, against, and apart from a world that changes. For Whitehead, an understanding of God as apart from and over the world infuses history with violence and over-againstness, especially when change swirls around. Whitehead's work alters the characterization of a God who is sovereign and distant from the world and replaces it with powerful proximity and mutual influence between created and Creator.

In process theology, we first understand that God is intimately part of the world. And God's power is not a power separate from the world at play to control us. God's power, in process thought, is relational power. God has the capacity to influence *and be influenced* by every single event and occasion taking place throughout the world and throughout time. Divine power is God's power to be tenderhearted enough to feel everything, every event, however minuscule or massive, and to be informed by and through that feeling. Powerlessness derives from apathy, i.e., the loss of feeling to which we are prone. Only God is strong enough to be tender to all the events in the world—good and bad—without succumbing to numbness. We are empowered through God to feel with and for the world.

How can God feel all of this, all of us, and not be overcome? God's ability to withstand being overwhelmed by all the feelings and needs of the world is the marked difference between us and God, one that is impossible to imitate. God can and does feel it all and remain close, collaboratively, and concerned. This capacity of God firmly roots a need for God in the systems of this world and cosmos. God's omnicompassion is the source of our living more justly and lovingly. Praying for a sense of God's tender heart can be a source of healing in a world plagued by self-indulgent actions of stone hearts.

Omnicompassion also renders God open to change and growth. Whitehead offers an image for this "operative growth of God's nature . . . that of a tender care that nothing be lost . . . a tenderness which loses nothing that can be saved."[8] In other words, God does not allow fear or pride to prevent change from happening. Change is part of life in God and life with God, and while we may worry and feel panic, God remains in touch with us. This is good news for us all as we navigate a time in history when change seems to be a weekly occurrence and stability can be so hard to find (and so appealing to cling to when we are worried and afraid).

Though Whitehead may not be a household name, Whitehead's proposals are woven into the work of a great many authors today (who are also more approachable): Diana Butler Bass and her horizontal grounded theology, for example, which has taken off in evangelical and mainline areas,[9] and organic church models that focus on the local and particular rather than general institutional church programs.[10] Thomas Jay Oord has also

---

8. Whitehead, *Process*, 346.
9. See Bass, *Grounded*.
10. See Cole, *Organic Church*; Ingram, *Organic Student Ministry*; Simson, *House*

translated the essence of process theology into open and relational theology for a broader audience in books like *God Can't: How to Believe in God and Love after Tragedy, Abuse, and Other Evils* and *The Death of Omnipotence and Birth of Amipotence.*

The primary difference between process and classic Western thought resides in an overly simplified phrase: *becoming*, not being. In other words, Whitehead "thawed out the metaphysical tradition of the West," as it was—frozen into eternal categories and facts—thereby "melting the unchanging" categories of substance and subject "into the turbulent flow of an endless Becoming."[11] According to Whitehead, no beings are ever static entities independent of the other non-static entities, or realities, or situations, or moments, from which they emerge. We never stop becoming, so long as we are living. We are human *becomings*, not merely human beings.

As keepers of the tradition of preaching in and for the church, it is easy to assume our task is preservation, not innovation. When we were forced to preach and lead worship online in March 2020, we likely first reached for platforms that allowed us to preserve the practices as we've been doing them rather than jumping into innovation. This makes sense theologically as well as practically. Christians often speak of God as a sustainer, so we think of God as the upholder of tradition. God is the great preserver of tradition, people, and church. But in process thought, God does not seek preservation as permanence. Rather, God helps creation persevere through change with a recognizable identity that is not exactly like it was before. Think of Jesus after the resurrection. He did not return the same as he was before he died and was buried. He bore the scars of his execution but also the radiance of resurrection; he was changed but the same.

And this is our invitation to engage the Gadfly, knowing God is with us in the conversation, to help us change preaching where we need to without losing our why and identity along the way. It is okay to change things! God is with us. We do not need to feel trapped in tradition so long as we hold onto the purpose for preaching, our *why*.

Church Book; Suttle, *Shrink*.

11. Keller, "Introduction," 10.

HOMILECCLESIOLOGY: ONE WORD TO CAPTURE THE WHY OF PREACHING

Whitehead also loved a neologism—that is, creating a new word when familiar words fail to convey a new idea that is coming forward. To break from philosophical predecessors, Whitehead felt the need to cultivate his own language occasionally. The new terms cause the listener to pause and seek understanding. The new terms unsettled unconscious and unchallenged norms regarding the way of the world and the way of God in and with the world. You might be a process theologian if you know terms he created, such as *concrescence, superject,* or *prehension.* To challenge philosophers to think differently, he used incomprehensible words!

Likewise, I propose the term *homilecclesiology* to make us stop and think about the *why* for preaching in a new way. Homilecclesiology—a hybrid of *homiletics* and *ecclesiology*—is a purposeful term for the events and energies present in the moment of preaching. Homiletics is the study of preaching. Ecclesiology, which contains the term *ekklesia,* is the study of the church in its multiple forms mentioned above. Blending the two terms to create a new term emphasizes that preaching contains more than rhetorical concerns about effectively communicating a message. Homilecclesiology interprets preaching as a beautiful and complicated entanglement of preacher, people, Scripture, Spirit, Word, church, tradition, situations, liturgy, sacraments, ecology, and God. And it also is the study of these entanglements.

Homilecclesiology is both a statement on "homiletical ecclesiology" and an "ecclesiological homiletic" in an era of ecclesiology that is shifting from reliance upon institutional affiliation and structure to networked ways of relationality, which we will discuss in upcoming chapters.[12] Preaching is always informational (instructing on Scripture, theology, tradition, etc.) and formational (shaping the body of Christ). Homilecclesiology is a term that shows concern for informational and formational aspects of preaching.

Homilecclesiology also contains the incarnational reality of preaching that we explored earlier in the chapter. According to Marjorie Hewitt Suchocki (also a process theologian), a "congregation is an organic body commissioned to do the work of Jesus Christ in the world."[13] In other

---

12. Allen, *Homiletic of All Believers,* 39.
13. Suchocki, *Whispered,* 29.

Why Bother Preaching?

words, preaching is a practice within the organic body that helps make Christ present in the church, and its task is never complete. As Suchocki so aptly described, preaching, "this mundane chore, this seemingly never-ending event—is today's equivalent of that stable, that manger," in which the revealed Word of God took his first breath.[14] Preaching incarnationally brings about God's incarnation in our time and place—the holy within the ordinary and organic matter of life. This is *why* we hear and practice preaching.

As we move through these chapters and discuss ways to play with and engage the Gadfly of new media and technology, let us look at preaching through this lens: at its best, proclamation about the good news revealed through Jesus Christ—his incarnation, life, death, and resurrection—emerges through in intentional gatherings of vulnerable, fragile, beautiful human beings seeking to live their lives aligned with this message. Preaching is in service of and an embodiment of the good news that God is still present and active in our world *through human beings.* Preaching is not merely done for fun or because it is an interesting hobby. Preaching is not theological Ted Talk-ing about God as revealed in Scriptures—sharing interesting tidbits about God who acted in the past. Preaching is not meant to highlight and recast all the bad news we see all week on the television and in our Newsfeed without aiming toward some promise that the "as is" is not the "as it should be." Preaching has good news within it and puts the good news in us. As homiletician Gennifer Brooks reminds us, preaching "enlivens, awakens, and energizes the preacher and people for joyful living even in a troubled world."[15] This is our *why*!

We bother to preach because it's a practice that animates the body of Christ through encounters with God's living Word so that we can live in a world that could be but is not yet in existence. The *why* does not revolve around everybody else doing it or because it's what the kids are into. Preaching is the ordinary means by which the extraordinary Word of God continues to become incarnate in and *for* the world's transformation.

---

14. Suchocki, *Whispered*, 17.
15. Brooks, *Good News*, 5.

Engaging the Gadfly

HOW WE PREACH AND WHY THAT MATTERS

In *The Art of Gathering*, Priya Parker critiques conversations about how we gather that only address "the stuff" on the surface.[16] Many books and webinars in this time of the Gadfly and technological shifts predominately address the surface of online preaching: choosing the right streaming platforms, setting up Facebook groups or pages, buying the right podcast microphones, and social media strategies. This is "stuff." These are "things." Only addressing "things" keeps us busy with items we can control (the *how*) without reflecting on the *why* of the *how*—the *why* being connection to one another and experiencing transformation in our gathering (whew, that's a mouthful). The stuff and things of *how* only matter *when connected to our why*. I wanted to start with the *why* so that we can be more imaginative and discerning with the *how* of preaching in this digital age.

How we go about preaching varies depending on our tradition, culture, context, language, and situation. For example, it would be ineffective for me to prepare to deliver a spoken message for the Deaf Liberty Baptist Church. The *how* of sermon delivery in that congregation is American Sign Language (ASL) because that is the congregation's language, and preaching is meant to be understood by those who gather around it.

Perhaps you are in a congregation that has invested in tools that allow you to livestream the sermon from the sanctuary on Sunday. The *why* for this was a mixture of local protocols informed by the Center for Disease Control and a desire for worship to not harm those gathering on Sunday morning. During the early months of the COVID era, you and a handful of leaders were in the sanctuary while the congregation stayed at home. But the *whys* of your online presence are different today. Should the *how* of livestreaming to an unseen and unknown gathering that may or may not be tuning in stay in place? In other words, should we continue to livestream the sermon when most of the congregation is back in the sanctuary?

Perhaps you are in a congregation that was small enough to pivot to an all-Zoom format for worship during 2020. While bumpy at first ("Barb, we can hear you talking to your phone . . . Don, we can see you walking into the bathroom"), eventually, the *how* of preaching (Zoom) allowed for more interaction and for the community to not only see the preacher's face but one another's in the preaching event. Now, back in the sanctuary, you've returned to a preaching style that centers the preacher in the pulpit,

---

16. Parker, *Gathering*, xi.

ending the more conversational moments that had begun to characterize preaching online. Some people miss the Zoom worship time, believe it or not! Why do you think that is? Perhaps the *how* of the pandemic has led to a new *why*.

Our experiences with emerging technologies and new media raise new questions about preaching through the lens of homilecclesiology:

- Is our preaching rooted in and expressive of the incarnation?
- Is our preaching for particular humans and developed by particular humans for a particular moment?
- Is our preaching helping us embody the Word revealed through Jesus Christ more holistically in our time and place?

Our answers to these questions shift our attention from the *why* of preaching, one that transcends time and shifts in culture, to the *how* of preaching, which brings us back to culture, context, and time.

SUMMARY

The Gadfly's buzzing allowed us to reflect on why we bother to preach. The concept of the Gadfly was introduced as a metaphor for the persistent questioning of established norms and practices within institutions. The chapter advocates for a deeper exploration of the *why* behind preaching before addressing the *how* of technological advancements and cultural shifts. The *why* offered is rooted in incarnation.

This chapter also introduced process theology, which helps us see God as with us through change rather than apart from it. Using Priya Parker's *The Art of Gathering* as a jumping-off point, this chapter challenged the notion of perpetuating practices solely based on tradition to stress the importance of understanding the theological and formational reasons behind preaching.

Holding on to what is essential about the why of preaching does not mean that preaching, worship, and the ways in which we are the church will not experience radical change. You may want to flip back a few pages to the quotes that opened this chapter. Why do you think I selected these in particular? Even if we dress up preaching in new media, we need to also let the Gadfly prompt us to ask whether or not this enterprise also requires "a new wearer of the clothes." We all may be invited to change-shift-transform our ideas, souls, and behaviors as we engage the Gadfly.

I proposed the term *homilecclesiology* to encapsulate the intertwining of preaching (homiletics) and the understanding of the church (ecclesiology). Homilecclesiology emphasizes that preaching involves more than effective communication of theology; it is about embodying the good news and nurturing the faith community, which is lived and living theology. It also challenges the notion that the church is a building. Rather, "church" describes what happens when individuals gather and congregate to hear and proclaim the good news.

In the coming chapters, we will continue to reflect on the purpose and significance of preaching and consider its theological underpinnings and relevance in a rapidly changing world influenced by technology and culture. This chapter set the stage for further exploration of how preaching can *adapt and thrive* in the digital age while remaining rooted in its fundamental purpose: transforming the world into a place of abundance, justice, and joy.

In chapter 2, we will look more closely at the historical relationship between technology and preaching, specifically in moments of shift. You'll hear me say throughout this book, *where there is shift, there is Gadfly*. The good news is that the church has seen and lived through many a "shift" before.

CONVERSATION PROMPTS:

1. Reflecting on your own experiences, why do you believe preaching is integral to Christian worship?

2. How do you think the wordy nature of our world today affects the impact of preaching? Do you find it challenging to cut through the "noise" and engage with sermon messages?

3. The chapter suggests that following tradition without understanding the underlying reasons may lead to disconnect. Have you ever questioned the purpose or relevance of preaching in today's context? Where did those questions lead you?

4. What are your thoughts on the concept of the Gadfly as a metaphor for questioning established norms within institutions? Do you think it's important for churches to engage in self-reflection and adaptation?

5. Reflect on practices around preaching that were created in response to COVID-19 in 2020. What did your congregation do to keep gathering around proclamation? What insights about the purpose of preaching did you gain from that season?

2

We've Seen This Shift Before

The Gadfly in Protestant Preaching Reformation(s) and Print Technoculture

I MET UP WITH my expat friend Maria while traveling through England. Though we'd only met in person one time five years prior, our connection was maintained and strengthened through social media, Instagram specifically. "We are Insta-friends!" she proclaimed as we greeted each other in Royal Leamington Spa.

From brunch, we went to a pub for gin and tonics and theological conversation. After all, we had much to discuss—she, a post-Christian writer and thinker, and I, a process theologian and new media scholar pushing the limits of what counts as preaching. In addition to the dance of ideas, we share roots in Catholicism and evangelicalism in our stories. From these roots shoots forth a shared love for wandering in holy spaces of worship to discover the historical and theological clues they hold.

Finding a church or cathedral in any city center in England doesn't take long, so we made our way to All Saints from the pub. Typically, these buildings are open, but we didn't seem to be in luck that day. We wandered around the towering façade, eyes drawn up, as we looked for an open door. Then we spied a man, Douglas, entering a wee side door. "Is the chapel open today?" Maria asked. "Well, it is now. Come on in!" replied Douglas.

We stepped through a closet/pastoral office and into the worship space. Eyes drawn up yet again. These neo-Gothic sanctuaries are meant to

We've Seen This Shift Before

do this, after all. The design itself is a technology to draw eyes, minds, and souls up into the heavenly realms and away from the burdens of this world.

"Would like to see the bells?" It turned out that Douglas was a bell ringer for the church. He had been ever since he was confirmed in the eighth grade and was told, "You are a full member of the church now! Time to take on a job! We have many positions." And he chose the bells—another technology of worship.

The ropes on the first landing almost appeared like a chandelier or intricate spider web overhead. Douglas asked us to step to the side and not pull on any ropes, warning that the untrained ringer could end up with a nasty rope burn at best and a mighty bump on the head at worst, if they underestimated the power of the machinery.

"Do you know anything about square dancing?" This is how Douglas explained the choreography required for full-circle bell-ringing for certain occasions and tunes. Full-circle tower bell ringing, or change ringing began in England in the seventeenth century. Each ringer is a note in a song. One ringer, however, is required to take on more memorization to conduct the music or call the change. The practice is necessarily communal, a dance in the round.

Church bells had been in use long before the seventeenth century. By 600 AD they were commonly found in monasteries, though they were introduced to churches in 400 AD. Before timekeeping was mechanized, universalized, and individualized, bell ringing was first and foremost communal and local. The bells announced the time, the pattern, and the events of each day.

The Reformation, as well, sparked innovation in church bells. The iconoclasts destroyed anything "ringing" of Catholicism, thus destroying many bell towers. When the dust settled, the sixteenth century space was made to utilize the latest technology—to mount bells on a full wheel. Now, the ringers could control the bells better, starting and stopping at will.

The church bells told the people it was time for worship. They told the people—"they" being the tellers or tailors with their bells, through death knell technology—when a member of the community was dying or had died, their gender (three times three strokes for male, two times three strokes for female) and age (one time three strokes for a child and a chime for each year the deceased lived).

During World War II, a decree silenced all church bells except to warn of enemy invasion. Imagine that shift in soundscape: to go from life when the bells consistently rang to tell time and call to worship, to a haunting silence in which the sound of those very same bells communicated warning instead.

Off to the side, in a corner of the landing, was a flat wooden box, also with ropes up to the bells on the next landing.

"What's that?"

"Oh, it's the Ellacombe apparatus," and Douglas explained this technology that enabled one person to ring the bells. The Ellacombe Chiming Frame was invented by Rev. Henry Thomas Ellacombe around 1821. At the time, bell-ringers were getting a reputation for having a wee bit too much alcohol-infused fun in their circles, so one trusted ringer seemed more efficient than getting a group of tipsy people together to ring them on time and in rhythm.

"We don't use it," Douglas said. "It just doesn't have the same sound." Then he opened the frame, nearly dropping a bottle of whiskey tucked inside the unused technology. "Oh, pretend you didn't see that!" Once, it was a technological innovation meant to streamline the work of bell ringing for an individual. Now it's just a cabinet for the celebratory libations of the ringers.

We've lived through shifts before.

All around your worship space are ebenezers of liturgical change. In the States, it's more likely that projectors, screens, and TV/VCR combos will be used in youth rooms. Some might even call hymnals ebenezers of change, as more congregations move to modern music or projecting music and lyrics onto screens.

Change is natural. Organic to our lives. Organic to worship.

Organic to preaching.

We've seen these shifts before, and we will see them again. And God accompanies us through them all. Each generation must ask how we will greet and engage them with intention and integrity.

PREACHING IN THE EARLY CHURCH

Preaching emerged from the influence of Jewish practice. In the synagogue, the reading and interpreting of the Law was the "centre of gravity" of the service.[1] Jesus' first recorded sermon in the Gospel of Luke is an example of this form of preaching, as he opens to Isaiah 61:1–2, reads aloud

---

1. Martin, *Worship*, 68.

We've Seen This Shift Before

in front of the gathering, returns to his seat amongst the gathering, and proclaims, "Today this scripture has been fulfilled in your hearing."[2] Only Jesus' so-called first sermon in Luke 4:16–30 occurs in the synagogue, a formal gathering event of Jewish people (like *ekklesia*, *synagogue* is a word that describes the action of people gathering and not simply a building for a gathering). Other than that, Jesus is portrayed in the Gospels as one who preaches in the everydayness of life. In homes and on the streets, he shared messages of varying length, messages interrupted by activity and questioning. These preaching events were often commentary on a concrete situation—live, in the moment, with application, and, at times, subversion of what the tradition (lawyers, Pharisees, prophets, history, Hebrew Bible) might have said. To arrive at insight, Jesus primarily asks questions and hosts the gathering in a theological dialogue with immediate application to the situation at hand. Out of the chaos of day-to-day life, Jesus spoke, provoked, listened, and responded, and new possibilities emerged as people gathered around the living Word.

This dialogical way of preaching in the community also has resonance with a philosophical form of *symposia* in Greco-Roman culture. While we may think of a lectern when we hear *symposia*, associating the word with contemporary symposiums that center on forty-five minutes of monologue followed by Q&A, *symposia* meant something else in the culture of the early church. The word means "drinking together" in Greek. Some forms of *symposia* centered on dialogue around a theme or topic, not an expert's lecture. Next time you come across a text in Luke where Jesus is reclining at a home, notice that it is often an event that has previously taken place in the assembly that prompts him to offer commentary and questions to the group, leading to shared reflection on morality and religion.[3] Is this preaching?

My predecessor at Saint Paul School of Theology, Mike Graves, raises a similar question in his book *Table Talk: Rethinking Communion and Community*. This book explores the role of meals in the early church's worship, including preaching. The *why* behind these gatherings reflects "the very nature of God and the gospel itself—intimacy, inclusion, festive joy, and participation in community."[4] The meal gathering and subsequent "table talk" occurred daily, not only on Sunday. Is table talk preaching?

---

2. Luke 4:21, NRSV.
3. Smith, *From Symposium to Eucharist*.
4. Graves, *Table Talk*, 8.

In the Acts of the Apostles, we see examples of missionary preaching and proclamation from wandering, itinerant preachers. They preached on busy streets, in homes, and around the temple. We cannot find evidence of *liturgical* preaching as we know it until the middle of the second century.[5] Eventually, the synagogal gathering around the reading and interpretation of the word synthesized with the banquet meal; as Christianity became the official religion of Rome and was no longer forced underground, the liturgy of Word and Table we recognize today was formed.[6]

Imagine the shift in preaching practice required as house churches (small, crowded, intimate, with low ceilings, domestic) gave way to basilicas (large, grand, with high ceilings, airy, imperialistic) in the fourth century. The liturgy shifted as the Christian movement was amplified and embraced by the Roman Empire instead of muffled and restrained as an odd mystery cult. Proclamation went from spontaneous conversations around the dinner table to the official message delivered from the bishop's chair set in the apse in order to project the sound into the narrow, long nave.

New technologies emerge. New motivations. New technoculture. And preaching changes.

Even a more recent look into the history of preaching, including Protestant preaching in my tradition of the Christian Church (Disciples of Christ), reminds us that preaching was once more commonplace than a weekly event. Writing about the early years of preaching in the Stone-Campbell movement, Dwight E. Stevenson claims that our forefathers "preached so often as to astonish us," with two or three different sermons on Sunday along with daily sermons in some Reformed communities.[7] John Wesley, in his journal from 1739, documents a typical week in the life of a frontier preacher: in the morning, preaching in one town, then in the evening, reading another Scripture and preaching on it in a different town.[8] Each day, another town, another sermon. Such was field-preaching in Europe and the colonies almost three hundred years ago. Wesley followed this pattern for fifty years of his ministry, only cutting down to one sermon a day when his sight began to decline.[9]

---

5. White, *Brief History*, 35.
6. Senn, *Christian Liturgy*, 54.
7. Stevenson, *Disciples Preaching*, 19.
8. Curnock, ed., *Wesley's Journal*, 72.
9. Curnock, ed., *Wesley's Journal*, 415.

We've Seen This Shift Before

All that to say, preaching has changed over time—from the *who* to the *when* to the *how* to the *where*. Preaching has not always and only been a monologue set within Sunday morning liturgy in a sacred building. Yet the compelling *why* does not always change: to continue a centuries-long practice of gathering, because preaching is the ordinary means by which the extraordinary Word of God continues to become incarnate in and *for* the world's transformation. This memory could help us stretch our imagination for the who, what, where, and how of preaching in our social media technoculture.

In the rest of the chapter, we will focus more on the Gadfly of print technoculture and how the rummage sale five hundred years ago impacted the church in the West. This is because the print age has standardized much of Protestant worship and preaching in the West. Part of the discomfort we feel as the Gadfly of social media and AI (Artificial Intelligence) buzzes around us is related to the shifting norms from print/broadcast/mass media to new social media. These norms create a technoculture that people swim in. What follows is a peek into how print came to shape preaching in the past, which will help us reflect and respond to how new media are shaping our present—without letting go of our *why* for preaching.

DEFINING TECHNOCULTURE

Often, the first place our mind goes when one asks about the relationship between worship and technology is the *artifacts* of technology. Artifacts are things like screens, computers, projectors, lights, etc. As we saw in chapter 1 with Priya Parker, these are the "stuff" related to the *how* of the gathering that erroneously gets more attention in planning than the *why* of a gathering.

According to Susan J. White, writing on technological innovation in Christian worship, the artifact and utility level of technological conversations is only one of three "distinct, but interpenetrating, levels" of technology.[10] Technology also refers to the processes by which artifacts are manufactured and the larger cultural attitudes that emerge as we influence and are influenced by technological change. These interactions between and through artifacts and people create particular *technocultures* for each age.[11]

10. White, *Christian Worship*, 16.
11. White, *Christian Worship*, 16.

Throughout this book, *technoculture* will be used as a term that encourages us to look beyond merely the artifact level (how) in order to engage the Gadfly of our digital age in levels impacting and impacted by cultural shifts (platforms, cameras, AI, etc.). The artifacts (technologies, tools) we fashion are fashioned from some motivation within us as humans, and something theological is embedded in those motivations. And the more we become accustomed to using particular tools in our religious practice, the more a particular culture—that is, a system of values, beliefs, morals, habits, language, and ways of being human—emerges.

According to White, mainline traditions, *especially* in the United States, are naïve about the impact of technology on how the liturgy is performed and prepared. Liturgy and technology have always had "something to do with each other" beyond the anachronistic question of "how to run the overhead projector."[12] However, the study of liturgy as an organized discipline in theological education has centered its energies on the retrieval of mythical culturally unscathed forms of prayer and order, or the text of earliest precedence and so of greatest authority regarding how liturgy should be done today, with little attention to the culture from which it emerged.[13] Certainly the study of preaching, homiletics, has operated under the same assumption at times, seeking to restore the practice by doing exactly what the early church did, as if a return to a pre-Empire praxis will renew the church today. White critiques this collusion of antiquity with orthopraxis (a theological word for right or best practice), arguing that it has distracted scholars from reflection on the technoculture of participants in the liturgy today, as well as from acknowledging how the original liturgy or preaching practice was itself a product of a particular technoculture.[14]

To offer examples of where technological change and liturgical change have intersected, White highlights time-keeping technologies as they developed—from the exactitude of calendars to hours and eventually, minutes and seconds, which directed the ringing of the bells of the opening story—as well as communication technologies such as the monastic scribe and printing press I will discuss below. Each tool—and the desires accompanying them before and because of their existence—changed worship practice *and* the perception of the people who participate in worship.

---

12. White, *Christian Worship*, 10.
13. White, *Christian Worship*, 28.
14. White, *Christian Worship*, 31.

We've Seen This Shift Before

Every age, White emphasizes, is a technological age with a unique technoculture.

We are not the first. And we will not be the last.

Every stage of Christianity has impacted and been impacted by the technologies of its age, especially as tools for mediation. Peter Horsfield, professor of communication at RMIT University who since 1984 has written on the relationship between media and Christianity, sees "Christianity itself as *a mediated phenomenon,* one in which the matrix of mediation within which it takes shape at any particular period of history is integral to its character."[15] Yet it would be wrong to claim that Christianity responded in unison to its emergence at any given period and with any given media. Local gatherings embody their *why* for mediating Christianity in ways that are like no other, like some others, and like all others. Discernment is required.

So it will be for us today as we respond to new media, Artificial Intelligence, and other shifts caused by our engagement with technologies and the technoculture we create and dwell in. This is why a conversation is central around why and how to engage the Gadfly locally. Our responses to shifts have not been and will not be uniform.

In her groundbreaking book, White never delves into the specifics of preaching and its relationship with technological media change. Such a survey has yet to be conducted. Yet a peek into works in homiletic history reveals how technology has influenced the content (the structures for argumentation expected in literate technoculture five hundred years ago up to Eugene Lowry's "loop" and its relationship to the sitcom of the 1980s) and delivery of the sermon (from basilicas, cathedras and cathedrals, triptychs, stained glass, printing press, and electronic sonic amplification). Our intentional, thoughtful, and critical relationship with changes in technoculture is vital to the impact of our ministry of the living Word.

Now we will learn an important mantra that shapes the rest of this book: *technology is not good, bad, or neutral.* This paraphrase is the foundation of the work of Melvin Kranzberg, a historian of technology. We will spend a few moments listening to Kranzberg's Laws to help us engage the Gadfly of technology reflectively, and not just reactively.

---

15. Horsfield, *From Jesus to the Internet,* 286.

FOUNDATIONS FOR TECHNOLOGICAL CONVERSATION: KRANZBERG'S LAWS

There is a tendency to approach technological change from one of two sides: obsessive fear or love. The obsessive fear side is described in research as "technological determinism," or technophobia. This is often the posture those who see an unavoidable future wherein our machines will overpower humanity, dehumanize us, and program *us* in machinelike fashion and/or erase our species from the planet. Gulp. (The rise of the chatbots!) Susan White summarized technophobia as the claim that technology is bound to control and limit human freedom as it grows beyond our control and imposes its own inorganic criteria onto organic life, thus dehumanizing and enslaving all it encounters.[16]

On the other side is technological embrace, or technophilia. This is the worship of technological development as if it is a tool for humanity to become perfect.[17] At its extremes, this approach assumes that we will eventually conquer death and the limits of our biological bodies with our brilliant technologies. Organizations embrace every new fad, platform, etc., just because it is new and better and will inevitably improve their life, regardless of whether it aligns with their mission, purpose, and why. Sometimes, you might see the word *posthumanism* or *transhumanism* used in these conversations. Posthumanism is often used in a broad manner and conflated with the telos of transhumanism (transcending humanism—sounds a lot like gnosticism to me). The key distinction between the two for the purposes of this project is that transhumanists are technophiles who tend to interpret cultural posthumanism by projecting a time in the future when, thanks to our advances in science and technology, we will as humans be *able to become posthuman*, that is able to transcend the limits of our biological bodies and be "reformulated" as humans, perhaps even becoming "ultra-humans."[18]

This may sound like science fiction to you, but when was the last time you stopped to consider how many of us have implanted technological software that helps us transcend limitations? Hearing aids, artificial limbs, and pacemakers are just a few examples of commonly accepted technological devices that help transcend biological limitations.

---

16. White, *Christian Worship*, 23.
17. White, *Christian Worship*, 23.
18. Ferrando, "Posthumanism."

We've Seen This Shift Before

Neither of these poles—technophobia or technophilia—is a generative starting place for us as we begin to think about how preaching and technology interact with one another and shape the church. Melvin Kranzberg presents a third approach to technology throughout his four decades of research and teaching.[19] A pioneer of the historical study of technology and the study of history through technological change, Kranzberg was the Callaway Professor of the History of Technology at the Georgia Institute of Technology. He was also one of the founders of the Society for the History of Technology and an editor of the journal *Technology and Culture*. In his 1985 presidential address to the society, Kranzberg summarized three decades of work with six laws framing the discipline of the history of technology. Here, we will examine a few of them more closely.

This section began with Kranzberg's First Law: technology is not good, bad, or neutral.[20] We've already discussed how brushing off technology as inherently evil or embracing all of it as good does not serve us well. But now we have a new concept: technology is not neutral! At all times, reflection or the spiritual practice of discernment about our use of technology and the emerging technoculture we exist within is required. What seems good about technology at the moment may end up having dire consequences on the ecology of our world. At the same time, technology that might initially seem bad may offer some good in the long run. What is the impact of technology on real bodies? On creation? This is what Kranzberg encourages us to consider together. Thus, it is the work of historians to pay attention to these trajectories and to educate those who make policy.

What is the work of theologians, then? I use that term expansively. I do not reserve it for people with degrees who teach in the academy. If you are reading this book, you are someone who is making sense of God, Jesus, Spirit, church, and human purpose/meaning. That's theological work! We

---

19. Christian ethicist Ian Barbour also takes the contextual approach to his work on the relationship between technology and religion, especially in his 1990 Gifford Lectures. Barbour admits that technology is a powerful force. It is a force for good and bad. It can liberate and threaten human life. It has evolved to address issues of global hunger and poverty and it has evolved as an agent of global climate change and nuclear war. Humans have power to do good and bad in this world with emerging technologies. It is a risky endeavor, for we are all part of one fabric, and face consequences that may have ripple effects beyond our immediate comprehension. Like Kranzberg, Barbour reaches the conclusion that we have the responsibility to identify and reflect over and again what is being imposed by technology and how we can modify it for the well-being of people and planet through political processes.

20. Kranzberg, "Technology," 545.

can appropriate Kranzberg's posture for ourselves as we discern how to preach into and within an age of chatbots and social media. Homilecclesiology means we reflect on technology as it impacts both the preaching practice and its impact on the congregation's faith formation.

Another theme in Kranzberg's scholarship is that technology has always been a human activity—fundamentally so—not merely an accessory to our development. It is no surprise that Kranzberg's fifth law elevates his life's work: while all of history is "relevant," according to Kranzberg, "the history of technology is the most relevant."[21] We need not say much more about this law here—only that it reminds preaching scholars of the importance of looking at how our tools of communication have impacted more than the means of delivering the gospel message.

Related is Kranzberg's sixth law. Anthropologists and archeologists insist that "the physical development of our species is apparently inextricably bound up with cultural developments," toolmaking being as fundamental as language development and abstract thinking.[22] Our becoming is intimately tied to how and why our tools become. But the becoming and emerging capacities of technology *do not determine* human actions.[23] Humans can and should decide and discern how they engage with their technologies. They can see in part how long-term effects harm or help social and political landscapes, and then right wrongs or encourage the good.

Technological skeptics may claim that when he delivered this address in 1985, Kranzberg could not have anticipated the advances in robotics and Artificial Intelligence that we have seen recently. Could his claim, "Behind every machine, I see a face—indeed, many faces: the engineer, the worker the businessman or businesswoman" stand today?[24] I think so. As advanced as we are, one look at even the most prestigious robotics competitions reveals the community of human intellect and ingenuity behind one robot's movements. One also sees how humans still need to step in when a part fails, when a robot gets off course, and when communication between the human mind and machine is broken. We are still years away from independent, self-healing robotic machines. The "software" (humans) still runs the "hardware" (machines).[25] But that does not mean the hardware isn't shaping us in return—far from it.

21. Kranzberg, "Technology," 553.
22. Kranzberg, "Technology," 557.
23. Kranzberg, "Technology," 559.
24. Kranzberg, "Technology," 558.
25. Kranzberg, "Technology," 558.

We've Seen This Shift Before

In summary, historians of technology such as Kranzberg strive to reveal how "utopian hopes" for technological innovation compared to "the spotted actuality."[26] It is the historian's duty to compare short-term aims with long-term results. Historians challenge notions of technological omnipotence and apathy regarding the role of technology in our world and our becoming. We are invited into a proactive stance, with our *why* for preaching in mind and heart, so that we can respond, utilize, and engage technologies with integrity and purpose and with an eye to the good of future generations.

In what follows, we will glimpse the emergence of the Gadfly five hundred years ago, when the last "great rummage sale" took place with the introduction of print technology and a new technoculture. It may comfort us that our ancestors lived and worshiped through complex shifts before us that radically changed how we learn, communicate, and relate to one another. Before we spend time with the Gadfly of the internet, Artificial Intelligence, and new media, let's see how the church encountered the Gadfly of the printing press and the shift to mass communication.

LOOKING BACK: THE GADFLY OF PRINT TECHNOCULTURE

> "The changes required of England's parishes during the reign of Edward VI were aimed at replacing a visual Christianity—belief understood through images—with belief conveyed through words."[27]

I often wonder what it was like to be a Christian in England in the two decades of rapid reform that led to the establishment of Henry VIII's Church of England. (Not normal thoughts, but hey, I am a professional worship nerd.)

England was one of the later Western holdouts of ecclesial reform, separated as it was from the continent and its buzz of reform in the Catholic Church. What buzz? Names dart and circle around the tradition like gadflies: Erasmus, Wycliffe, Hus, Lefevree . . . and the machine contributing to new ways of thinking and communicating—the printing press. The

---

26. Kranzberg, "Technology," 558.
27. Ives, *Reformation Experience*, 189.

Reformation was really a combination of many reforms, not just about practice and dogma in the church.

The Bible was translated into German and French before it was translated into English. Translating the Bible into English had been banned since 1409 (what was their fear?). William Tyndale was an outlaw simply because he undertook the translation project and cooperated with printers outside of England to make the word of God accessible to his fellow English speakers. In October 1536, after being lured from his safe house in Antwerp, Tyndale was strangled and burned for his law-breaking behavior.[28] His final shout: "Lord, open the king of England's eyes."[29]

And, wouldn't you know, shift happened. Within two years, every church in England and Wales was required to have a copy of the once-banned English bible—the *Great Bible*—in their possession for public reading. And who made it so? Orders came from King Henry VIII, whose eyes indeed were opened.

So, imagine worship in England around 1520. As a priest, your job was to lead the prescribed ritual drama of the Mass in Latin. Your back was to the people for the critical moment, the ringing of the sacring bell and elevation of the host. You rarely preached. When you did preach, you might have a book of homilies in Latin to read. Scriptures were also read to the people in Latin. Even from an elevated pulpit or lectern, it was unlikely that the people could hear you, let alone understand you. And before printing, it was rare for any individual to own a bound collection of Scriptures for themselves. The Holy Bible was mediated through the Mass via the priest and other officers in leadership.

Now imagine worship in England around 1520 as a layperson. The mass was a sensual event, layered in smells, movements, sounds, and sights that created an atmosphere of worship and devotion that held your senses and kept you safe from an outside world of plague, hunger, violence, and exposure to the elements. You do not know Latin. But that's not vital to participating in worship. It was still deeply incarnational, even without words that could be translated and understood clearly. You have been raised in the parish, so while you cannot understand the words sung over you and around you, you certainly have an embodied understanding of the choreography of the Mass, especially that moment when the ordinary elements become for us, oh what a miracle, the body and blood of Jesus Christ!

28. Ives, *Reformation Experience*, 140.
29. Daniell, *William Tyndale*, 382–83.

We've Seen This Shift Before

The Gadfly of shifts in technoculture started buzzing long before 1517 when a German monk named Martin Luther, seeking Catholic Church reform, posted ninety-five theses to a door. But thanks to the timing of his action, Luther went whatever the equivalent of "going viral" was, and his messages, called "flying writings," were picked up, translated, and printed across Europe. His *why* revolved around access to God for ordinary people—through participation in communion, Scriptures read and heard in the language of the people, and leadership that was organic to the local parish and not sent over from Rome. Buzz, buzz, buzz.

Luther was an incredibly media-savvy priest who fully engaged the newest media to spread his sermons and teachings of the movement in the language of the people. This included the use of comedic images to belittle his opponents. Rather than only being confined to church councils and communicated in the language of business at the time—Latin—these debates and theological fights among reformers and traditionalists were printed in pamphlets and distributed for all who were literate to see. For the illiterate, cartoons were also printed, mocking one side or the other and fanning the flames of reform. In the 1520s, as many as one million copies of Luther's pamphlets were circulating Germany, with a population of roughly six million at the time.[30]

If you think we invented the meme or trolling in our social media age, think again. Images like the one on the next page were created and distributed widely to mock opponents and communicate with an illiterate population. Lucas Cranach, the Elder, created the image "The Papal Belvedere" for Martin Luther's *Depiction of the Papacy* (1545). Why on earth are these two men, well, passing gas in the direction of Pope Paul III? The text roughly reads (because the Latin is unclear and mixed with Italian): "The Pope speaks: Our sentences are to be feared, even if unjust. Response: Be damned! Behold, o furious race, our bared buttocks. Here, Pope, is my 'belvedere.'" Belvedere, a word meaning "beautiful view," also refers to a building in the Vatican. Thus, these two German peasants are meeting Pope Paul III and his fire and brimstone papal bull with their own, shall we say organic, fire and brimstone.

---

30. Columbia University Libraries, "Flying Writings."

"The Papal Belvedere" by Lucas Cranach, the Elder, in the 1545 publication of Martin Luther's *Depiction of the Papacy.* [31]

By 1539, so much had changed for the average English priest and the layperson. Lifespans of course are not what they are today (another technocultural shift thanks to modern medicine, plumbing, clean energy, etc.), so maybe only a handful fully experienced just how dramatic a shift it had been. Of course, as in all reform, there was a spectrum of shift depending on how much was sold in the local church rummage sale and what was allowed to emerge in its place—from the evangelical reformers in England to those traditionalists who tried to maintain what they could of the Catholic liturgy. Nonetheless, the change, subtle and consistent over two decades, was swift in comparison to the centuries of practice before.

In May 1544, Thomas Cranmer's first church service in the English vernacular was published, and King Henry ordered that every parish use it by June.[32] The mysterious Latin words that underscored a mostly visual liturgy were now in common English. How did that impact the laity? I imagine them noticing, pausing, and seeking ways to be still and not only hear

---

31. "Papal Belvedere," Wikimedia Commons.
32. Ives, *Reformation Experience*, 151.

the sound of the priest's voice but also understand the words he was saying about God, Jesus, Scripture, hell, heretics, and everything in between.

Print technoculture's emergence led to shifts in the understanding of authority in the church as well. No longer were the pope and Rome the gatekeepers holding the authority and monies to finance and distribute hand-printed and illuminated sacred texts for use in churches across the empire. As presses popped up in different nation-states, the people chose to print in their local languages. Bit by bit, local press by local press, authority was becoming more localized in the protesting (Protestant) churches. And the word—in the local language of the people—was at the heart of the shift.

> The most powerful element in the reformed message was undoubtedly the proclamation of the Bible in English . . . The Bible gave preachers new authority. They were not repeating church dogma; they were expounding truth directly from the divinely inspired book in front of them . . . which anyone could access for himself if he could read or have someone read to him.[33]

No wonder King Henry, with his *Great Bible* in the English language for the first time, included a cover image of him distributing the word of God to the clergy and laity.[34] He appealed to the *scriptural word* as the head of the Church of England. Not Rome, not the pope. The word, printed, eternalized, inerrant, was king—even to the king.

Worship architecture reflected these shifts as well. Atmospheric spaces for worship in which the eye of the worshiper was drawn up into mosaics, windows, and gilded altars where the body of Christ dwells were replaced with Protestant architecture. Iconoclasts in some reformed spaces stripped the sanctuary of gold and anything that reminded them of Roman religion.

Why remove the kaleidoscope of religious imagery, smell, and liturgical drama? Because, for Protestant reformers, the Word of God was the presence of God—rightly preached and heard. *Sola scriptura* became the mantra as the church replaced papal authority with the authority of the sacred text. The center of focus was the lectern and pulpit. And pews were created so the worshipers could sit still and hear the saving word read and preached in their language.

Protestant Reformed traditions ran and walked with the shifts of print technoculture to respond to a reclaimed *why* (hearing and understanding the truth in holy Scripture through preaching) with new *hows*—redesigning

---

33. Ives, *Reformation Experience*, 170.
34. Ives, *Reformation Experience*, 140.

worship spaces to highlight the word read and preached by the pastor, arranging the laity neatly in pews to hear the word, printing Bibles, hymnals, and other devotional materials based on the word to guide the spiritual formation of the people.

Western Christianity since 1600 has been heavily impacted by print technoculture. At first, the buzz was a nuisance to the established order—moving away from the church's official language of Latin into many languages, churches then taking on the characteristics of their locality, including local governance, rather than Rome. The Catholic Church preserved its pattern, including Latin liturgy, into today. But they were no longer the only option for following the Way (and, of course, there were schisms before 1500 and already more diverse embodiments of the Way than our overly simplified history articulates!). These shifts also led to new ways of knowing, communicating, and relating to one another as a church that had been associated with oral/aural technoculture sprouted churches more closely associated with print/literacy technoculture.

Overall, print technoculture profoundly influenced Western Christianity, democratizing access to religious texts, shifting the focus toward individual interpretation of Scripture, and rearranging the furniture of the space where preaching and worship happened as well. It is hard for us to have the historical imagination to place ourselves in the shift from oral culture to print. We did not live in the shift! And now, we in the United States are, for the most part, so steeped in the shift to print and literacy technoculture that we know nothing else . . . that is until the Gadfly started to challenge us with the internet, social media, and Artificial Intelligence. Buzz, buzz!

ORALITY AND LITERACY: A SHIFT IN TECHNOCULTURE

Walter Ong, in *Orality and Literacy*, describes the impact of the shift from orality to literacy (print technoculture) on ways of knowing and relating to one another. One of the critical shifts Ong names was about how knowing occurs in societies. In oral/aural cultures, wisdom is passed down in conversation and story, taking place locally and rarely distributed more than ten miles from a city. Knowing was relational in oral technoculture, argues Ong, reliant upon the distance between an unamplified speaker and listener.

We've Seen This Shift Before

The early church was steeped in orality, as were the Jewish and Greco-Roman cultures that comprised the early church. Preaching was only ever done mouth to ear, except for the occasions when letters could be composed and sent. But even then, the letter was read aloud to a gathering, not meant to be read silently in the mind of an individual. Orality was a local, communal technoculture that emphasized proximity and story. Words shared were community-forming events.

With print technoculture, knowing could become universalized and standardized. The information gathered by one person in one place could be packaged and produced for everyone anywhere. With print came silent reading. Printed materials became more ubiquitous, and individuals could read words to themselves and by themselves, with no community required. Knowing, Ong argues, becomes abstract, universalized, and concrete, divorced from a particular time and place.[35] One of the critical aspects of print technoculture, according to Ong, is a "monopoly control over the expression of truth," in which "fewer and fewer hands" disseminate information for more and more people.[36] Expert hierarchies become deeply entrenched in church and society, even as information becomes more readily available to the masses.

Philip Clayton argues that a particular theology takes shape in technocultural shifts after the printing press. After Gutenberg, theologies of churches were produced and mediated through books, hymnals, and collections of prayers authorized by denominations seeking to form the faith of their community apart from other denominations. The church and its publication houses became trusted authorities in this system, distributing knowledge to various locations where the denomination had outposts. Christians would "consume" the theology from books and sermons from preachers whose theology was also shaped by the authorized books on doctrine and Scripture.[37] The print aspect of the technology lent a sort of timelessness to producing knowledge. Scriptures, printed and translated, become "inerrant." Doctrines of the church become truth dislocated from a particular voice, culture, and place of privilege. Theology becomes abstract, universal, and individualistic.

A certain homilecclesiology takes shape in print technoculture. A minister of the Word (and Sacrament) is needed to mediate the holy

---

35. Ong, *Orality and Literacy*, 42.
36. Hartley, "Before Ongism," 208.
37. See Clayton, "Theology After Google," and "Church After Google."

Scriptures correctly for the people. The preacher becomes the expert on reading and applying the printed word of God to the masses. Textbooks are printed, and academic experts writing these textbooks tell the pastor the correct interpretation of the sacred text (historically, socially, linguistically, and doctrinally). Education also involves training in rhetoric so that the message is clearly argued and the listeners receive *the* point of the message that the preacher has to deliver. Consider how modern homiletics and the design of Protestant theological seminaries have been entangled with these norms since the stabilization of the print age.

These reforms—shifts—were initiated and amplified when the Gadfly provoked critical reflection on the norms of preaching and worship. Only in time and through time did some realize that reforms meant to give more Christians access to the Word of God in Scripture and participation in worship had in some ways created more boundaries around the *who* and *how* of preaching that once relied upon proximity, intimacy, and participation in oral/aural technoculture (think back to the table talk of the early church . . . witnessing was not a paid role, was it?).

SUMMARY

In this chapter, we encountered stories and examples of shift and defined the word *technoculture*. We learned that where shift is, a Gadfly emerges to challenge our how and remind us of our why for organizing our lives in community. We were specifically introduced to the Gadfly of print technoculture in the European Reformation, which is the ecosystem in which more Protestants in the United States have worshiped, worked, raised families, etc., for five hundred years.

Now, the Gadfly of the digital age is buzzing. The buzz signals change. In the next chapter, we will focus on how homiletics, the study of preaching, has been unknowingly engaging this Gadfly, in the shift from print to digital mediation and technoculture. We leave the historical overview of the rummage sale five hundred years ago to focus on our current situation, stirring up unrest about inherited forms of preaching after Gutenberg: questions about the efficacy of a monological sermon. Does the ubiquitous form for preaching in the West inherited from print technoculture—a fifteen- to forty-five-minute message from one person delivered to many people—meet preaching's *why* for a people for living into the Way of Jesus in the twenty-first century? Some think this relic of the print, mass media, and broadcast technoculture needs reconsideration in the emerging era of social media.

CONVERSATION PROMPTS

1. Do you agree with Kranzberg's foundational law: technology is not good, bad, or neutral? Why or why not? Can you offer examples of each?
2. Do you agree that Christianity is inherently mediated by the technologies of each era? Why or why not?
3. Reflect on the evolution of preaching from its origins in Jewish practices to its present-day forms. How has technology influenced preaching styles and content?
4. Reflect on the change in preaching that took place when the worship service was in a language people could understand. What might be gained or lost in the shift from orality to literacy in worship?
5. Look at your worship space. What echoes of this historical overview do you see and experience in the building? Does it still align with the why for your tradition's ways of preaching and worship? Why or why not?

3

Communication Breakdown

Exploring the Pupal Stage of the Gadfly in the 1960s

> "I say beware of all enterprises that require new clothes and not a new wearer of the clothes." —Henry David Thoreau

IN CHIMAMANDA NGOZI ADICHIE'S 2009 TED Talk, "The Danger of a Single Story," she tells a story of what it was like for her only to read books about American and British characters as a young girl growing up in Nigeria. "The unintended consequence," Adichie says, "was that I did not know that people like me could exist in literature."[1] The people who served as gatekeepers and experts in publishing and producing stories for the masses chose characters who looked like them—often white, cisgender, European, or North American middle- to upper-class characters. The world was explored through their eyes—be it fiction or nonfiction.

After discovering African books, Adichie was "saved . . . from having a single story of what books are."[2] She began to push against the form of publishing and storytelling that had been established as she immersed herself in the words and worlds of non-white storytellers.

Traveling to the United States years later, Adichie experienced the danger of a single story again. She was nineteen and studying at an American university. Her roommate, an American, was constantly surprised

---

1. Adichie, "Single Story."
2. Adichie, "Single Story."

by her Nigerian roommate—she "spoke English so well" and listened to Mariah Carey instead of African "tribal music." Adichie continues, saying this about her naïve roommate:

> What struck me was this: She had felt sorry for me even before she saw me. Her default position toward me, as an African, was a kind of patronizing, well-meaning, pity. My roommate had a single story of Africa. A single story of catastrophe. In this single story there was no possibility of Africans being similar to her, in any way. No possibility of feelings more complex than pity. No possibility of a connection as human equals.[3]

While Adichie was saved from having a single story of what books are, she soon realized that the loudest and most ubiquitous story was still told through white, European, or North American voices. Part of Adichie's calling (why) is to challenge the presence of a single story in literature. Adichie writes novels as a Nigerian and from the complex ecosystem of her context. Adichie's TED Talk currently has over eighteen million views.[4]

Who has the power and authority to tell stories?

Who has the power and authority to preach us into God's story?

These questions sound like the buzz of the Gadfly as we address the shifts that are currently taking place as the dominance of print technoculture gives way to a digital age. These shifts will require more than new artifacts applied to old ways of preaching. They will require a new preacher and a new idea for being a congregant in the sermon event. Before we dive into a description of the emerging technoculture, we will spend time listening to voices in the twentieth century who challenged norms for preaching inherited by print and its evolution into broadcast and mass-mediated technoculture before the internet and social media. These were the pupal stages of the Gadfly, beginning in the 1960s and moving into the first decade of the twenty-first century.

FROM PRINT TO BROADCAST—MASS MEDIA AND THE SPECTATOR IN THE PEWS

The same sort of anxiety and fear that many share about our digital times emerged with the shifts in radio and television fifty years ago. As printers

---

3. MacFarquhar, "Adiche Comes to Terms."
4. MacFarquhar, "Adiche Comes to Terms."

and publishers organized and institutionalized religious materials, the seeds for the next shift became the soil of culture before the tools came into existence: broadcast. First, radio and then television brought attributes of print technoculture that rely upon one-to-many communication to new heights. And, again, preaching was impacted by these shifts in culture in ways we often take for granted. Megachurches, especially ones with satellites or campuses with the same preacher across all locations, are the clearest artifact of the broadcast technoculture's impact on Christian religious life. They engaged tools and technicians of the mass media world to increase their capacity for viewership in worship spaces, including televised spaces.

Mass media is a term coined in the early 1940s by Harold Lasswell, though it has been in existence as a phenomenon since the creation of the printing press.[5] Lasswell used the term in the context of government, and related the term to propagandistic activities on both sides of World War II. Mass media is the technical use of any media in order to (re)produce knowledge and information efficiently—reducing dialogical relations in order to amplify the mediated message at the expense of conversation.[6] Mass media is by nature a one-way message system privileging the distributor of the message. Distribution is not in the hands of the public. The flow of communication is top-down. The public is thus formed for receptivity and consumption of the message coming through the mass media pipeline.

A criticism of mass media technoculture was highlighted recently by Dan White Jr. in *The Act of Dialogical Preaching: The Convergence of Conversation & Proclamation in Public Discourse*. White highlights Jay Nash's 1932 neologism for the early broadcast era: "spectatoritis."[7] According to Nash, Americans' media habits were shaping a nation of onlookers, people who succumb to the easiest thing: watching somebody else do what they won't put the effort into learning how to do. He laments that while mechanization had opened more free time for people, they passively consumed theater and other media in the early twentieth century instead of participating in restorative activities.

White applies Nash's concern to the sermon: passively consuming sermons as a "spectator allows us to assemble in a room with others while keeping our individualism unchallenged."[8] I've written in the past about

---

5. Hardt, *Myths*, 15.
6. Hardt, *Myths*, 14.
7. Nash, *Spectatoritis*.
8. White, *Act of Dialogical Preaching*, 4.

similar concerns, specifically as it relates to print technoculture, mass media, colonization, and white supremacy in Christian expansion since the 1600s.[9] Seeker-friendly churches of the 1980s and 1990s adapted the technoculture of mass media and entertainment to draw people to church. Sermons were entertaining, and the event for preaching was intentionally designed to feel like attending a concert, comedy show, or sporting event where you are one among many with all eyes on the stage.

What happens when the spectatoritis of the arts and recreation is woven into the fabric of church? Remembering Kranzberg's first law from the previous chapter, what are mass media technology's good, bad, and non-neutral impacts on preaching? Let's explore!

COMMUNICATION BREAKDOWN

"Has modern preaching lost its old power?"[10]

This is the question Clyde H. Reid with which opens his 1963 article "Preaching and the Nature of Communication." Reid does not hold back his concern about the state of Christians, particularly American Protestants, in their daily lives. He laments that they do not articulate their faith in words or actions. He complains they are more captivated by advertisements and materialism than religious life. Reid says the inaction and apathy of Protestants in the world suggest that "Something is wrong with our current efforts to communicate the gospel of Jesus Christ."[11] He puts the blame squarely on the preaching practice of the American Protestant church, which relies upon outdated assumptions about how best to communicate a message to people.

For Reid, preaching as a form of communication is subject to the laws of human communication. These laws change over time and across places (he doesn't say it, but I'll say it—technoculture impacts communication). Reid questions the efficacy of preaching monologues as he reads the emerging scholarship about communications. Reid notes, "Until about 1950, communications researchers thought of communication chiefly as a simple, one-way process."[12] Under that paradigm, preachers and speakers poured attention into their argumentation, logic, and delivery without

---

9. Sigmon, "Preaching by the Rivers of Babylon."
10. Reid, "Nature of Communication," 40.
11. Reid, "Nature of Communication," 40.
12. Reid, "Nature of Communication," 41.

much concern for how the situation of the hearer impacts the reception and comprehension of a message. In seminaries, preaching was still taught as sacred rhetoric, engaging textbooks like John A. Broadus's *On the Preparation and Delivery of Sermons* (1870), which also operated under the paradigm of effective one-way delivery (hence the title). Following rules of rhetoric—creating spaces for one to speak clearly to the many—preaching will "work" in the church. However, Reid argued that new evidence disrupts these long-held paradigms. Dialogue, not monologue, is the most efficient way of communication.[13] For preaching to shape how Christians live in the way of Christ more effectively, sermons do not need better theological content or stories; they must break free from a "monological illusion" that leads preachers to believe that telling people what they should do will result in them doing what you say.

"Monological illusion" is a term Reid borrows from theologian Reuel L. Howe. Howe used the phrase to indicate "the concept that communication is accomplished by telling people what they ought to know."[14] Howe, a contemporary of Reid, also named a crisis in preaching. It seemed to Howe that a communication breakdown took place (perhaps this inspired the Led Zeppelin song?). The laity struggled to understand the preaching of the church in the tumult of the 1960s. And preachers struggled to translate the meaning of the gospel into the lives of their congregants. This situation and the limitations of monological preaching are at the heart of Howe's 1967 *Partners in Preaching: Clergy and Laity in Dialogue*.

How many times have you listened to a sermon from someone telling you what you ought to know? Here is a fun game for you to try: tally how many times you hear "should, ought, must" in the sermon next Sunday. Do you ever wonder what it might feel like to be asked a question? Not a rhetorical one, a real prompt that allows you to respond to what the preacher has proposed so far? And as a preacher, have you ever wondered what might happen if the congregation follows through on those *oughts, musts,* and *shoulds* that punctuate your sermon (especially when trying to land the plane at the end)? This prickly situation in which the preacher is supposed to know best how a diverse congregation lives out the gospel remains with us today. These phrases tied to the monological illusion are still pervasive in preaching over half a century after Howe's critique.

---

13. Reid specifically cites communications studies of Fearing, "Social Impact of Mass Media."

14. Howe, *Miracle of Dialogue*, 32.

Communication Breakdown

Under the monological illusion, we also assume that the preacher is the only trained expert who can approach the Scripture and tease out theological implications for the church. Reid does not bring print technoculture into his argument, but you might see now how print, mass media, and broadcast form and fit set the preacher apart from the congregation to deliver sacred messaging to the mass(es). As Broadus's title suggests, one needs only to correctly prepare and deliver the message. Hearers will accept it if done correctly.

However, new scholarship, such as the ones mentioned by Reid and Howe, challenged the efficacy and centrality of this communication model in the holy shifts of the 1960s that disrupted institutions throughout the United States with new ideas, perspectives, and technologies. Citing and paraphrasing the scholarship of Melvin L. DeFleur and Otto N. Larsen, Reid describes at least seven critical steps in the communication process (assuming comprehension and action are evidence of effective communication).[15]

1. Transmission occurs when the communicator presents their message.

2. Contact occurs when the listener has heard the message. *(This is where the teaching and practice of preaching usually ends; the work of the pastor is done, the congregation is left to receive the message.)*

3. When the listener is allowed to ask a question, comment, or otherwise express themselves concerning the message's content, feedback is established, and there is a *potentiality* for dialogue (note, feedback is not dialogue).

4. Having clarified their understanding, the listener now comprehends.

5. Having understood, the listener now accepts, ignores, or rejects the message.

6. Beyond simply accepting the message intellectually, the listener internalizes it when it becomes part of their being.

7. At this point, the communicator and listener have a shared common understanding and can act based on this understanding.

Most preachers focus on steps one and two and assume the other steps will occur after the sermon. However, for Reid, this error does not lead to dialogue. The impact for Reid is clear: "The absence of dialogue in the preaching situation may be the key to understanding the failure of

---

15. Reid, "Nature of Communication," 42.

preaching to achieve the results in changed lives."[16] Monological preaching does not create the sort of conflict, relational agility, and space to bring about transformation. Standing in the pulpit, with authority, to deliver a message without feedback beyond body language is easy and provides false comfort for the preacher and laity. But does it change lives? Reid is skeptical and so asks if the monological mode of preaching is valid any longer.

His conclusion is clear: "Preaching as an isolated event in itself is an insufficient vehicle for the communication of the gospel."[17] While he proposes a need to break free of the monological illusion, he ultimately decides it may be a fruitless task. Too many institutions are involved—too much risk. Too many shifts are required for preaching, preachers, and laity to break free of the inefficient but comfortable setup of the pulpit delivering a message to the pews.

The wallop at the end of Reid's essay comes in his section titled "Beyond Preaching." Here, he takes issue with paying professionals to preach. One person selected and paid to be the performer of the bulk of the church's ministry is, for him, the underlying problem of the church. In a primitivist move, Reid says, "In the early church there was no distinction of status between those who had the gift of preaching and those who had the gift of teaching or healing."[18] In other words, the hierarchy had not been set in place as it is today, with preaching elevated as the most important spiritual gift, the church putting money where the mouth is and not the hand, eye, knee, etc. (1 Cor 12:12–27). This development prevented shared ministry that empowers laity to witness through *their* gifts, and created an unsustainable office for the pastor. Reid continues, "By turning the preaching ministry over to a paid professional, we are also giving him a job too big for one man [sic] alone."[19]

For Reid, this presents a big problem for the pulpit. The why for preaching (changed lives) is not going to be accomplished by tweaking the how. He is calling for more than new clothes or artifacts to modernize the old form of preaching. Reid is calling for "a new wearer of the clothes," to reference an aphorism from Henry David Thoreau that opened this chapter. Preaching and preachers need to undergo radical change to break free of the monological illusion. The pastor *and* the laity need to embody

---

16. Reid, "Nature of Communication," 43.
17. Reid, "Nature of Communication," 47.
18. Reid, "Nature of Communication," 48.
19. Reid, "Nature of Communication," 49.

the ministry of the word differently. So long as the Protestant church is preacher-centric, no real change will occur in the lives of parishioners, according to Reid. The Protestant enterprise needs to be shaped in such a way as to allow for multiple voices, feedback, and the sharing of the gospel as it is known in their lives.

In summary, the monological illusion tells two lies. First, it operates under the lie that one-way communication is an effective way to effect change in the lives of Christians. Second, and related to it, is the lie that only clergy have the authority to translate scriptural truths into lived theology for the church.

After 1963, many homileticians began to address these shifts, calling for a "new homiletic" to help preaching engage the Gadfly as it emerged in the pupal form to challenge modernity's print-age conceptions of truth, authority, and preaching. I believe the late 1960s up until the early 2000s was the pupal stage for the Gadfly of the digital age. Signs of the need for a rummage sale were revealing themselves in the shift from modernism to postmodernism, black and white visual media to color, and a few channels picked up on an antenna to a cable package that expanded our avenues for entertainment and information away from a standard few options for all to many choices and niches to dwell in. This is the pupal state of a new technoculture that challenged monological illusions in more areas than preaching. The following brief exploration into homiletic efforts to break free of the monological illusion reveals how correct Reid's concerns were some sixty years later.

NEW HOMILETIC AND THE TURN TOWARD THE LISTENER

Out of the chaos of war, revolutions, flower power, cults, civil rights movements, and decline in church attendance, conversations about the need for a new hermeneutic for preaching began to emerge among homileticians. While the legendary preacher and scholar Fred Craddock is most often named the father of the movement, its reemergence in homiletics is partly thanks to David Randolph and his 1969 book *The Renewal of Preaching*.

Randolph claimed in the late 1960s that the church was experiencing a "rebirth of preaching ... amid the social upheavals of our time."[20] Preachers and churches were pivotal in leading civil rights movements. Randolph

---

20. Randolph, *Renewal*, 24.

urged the church not to let go of this revolution and go back to forms of preaching that were more focused on rhetorical order and abstraction than the why, or theology, behind the practice: transformation in the here and now. As Randolph said, preaching "is the pivot on which the Christian revolution turns. If we fail, then preaching may become the pit into which the Christian revolution falls."[21]

Randolph was critical of an era of preaching that focused more on the form than the theology of what happens in and through preaching (the why). Of particular blame was John A. Broadus (1827–1895), president of the Southern Baptist Seminary and author of *On the Preparation and Delivery of Sermons* (1870).[22]

> It was a fateful day when the venerable John A. Broadus asserted, in the work that was to become the standard in its field for generations, that homiletics was a branch of rhetoric. American homiletics has not yet been completely reconstituted after this stroke which severed the head of preaching from theology and dropped it into the basket of rhetoric held by Aristotle.[23]

Homiletics and theology are inseparable, according to Randolph. Yet, he said, because the standard method's *why* originated in rhetoric rather than theology, we need a new method for the Christian revolution to continue. Turning to biblical scholarship of the time, he brings the "new hermeneutic" of Gerhard Ebeling to homiletics. According to Ebeling: "The hermeneutic task consists for theology in nothing else but in understanding the *Gospel* as addressed to *contemporary man* [sic]," and while this produces tension, "Whoever does not expose himself to the tension that entails, betrays both—the Gospel and contemporary man alike."[24]

In other words, preaching is renewed by a new hermeneutic that relies upon the relationship between theology and people. Instead of only focusing on rhetoric and how to preach the text (Broadus's focus), preachers need to learn how to study the context in which the gospel proclaimed comes to life. The renewal of preaching comes through understanding, not ignoring, reality. Thus, Randolph asks, "whether the church will develop a

---

21. Randolph, *Renewal*, 25.

22. More needs to be said about the racism of Broadus, who was also a Confederate chaplain for Robert E. Lee and defended the validity of slavery. Did separating preaching from theology allow Broadus to ignore the dehumanization of chattel slavery?

23. Randolph, *Renewal*, 21.

24. Randolph, *Renewal*, citing Ebeling, 12–13.

homiletic worthy of the future which opens before it and thus assist preachers to rise to the occasion?"[25]

That's how we reach Randolph's proposal for a *why* from which a how will follow: "The homily must then be understood in its uniqueness as the form of discourse designed to bring the word of God to expression in the concrete situation of the hearers."[26]

Fred Craddock joined the conversation started by homiletician David Randolph by also asking how preaching could address the noticeable gap between what preachers want congregants to know and what is taking place in the world outside of the Bible. A "new homiletic" should be "designed to bring the word of God to expression in the concrete situation of the hearers"[27] in place of the old homiletic that "spoke but did not listen" to the situation of the people.[28]

Craddock argued that sermons had been fitted to a world celebrating the written word with certainty and logic, clear argument, and delivered from the authority of the clerical office. Preachers were authorities because they were adequately trained to use the best methods in sermon design and flow to transfer the message from the pulpit to the pew. (Remember that Craddock is talking about sermons from the modern print technoculture.) With the turn to print, truth itself became understood as something that could be fixed, abstract, and universally applied across contexts and times.

During the Enlightenment, theological education had become more formalized around a specific "encyclopedia" of knowledge: systematic theology, history, and biblical studies. The clergy in training was introduced to the latest and greatest information captured in books. For some Protestant preachers, the sermon content and form centered on teaching the congregation these facts about God. People living today mattered less than the historical context of the Scripture, dogmatics of tradition, and the rules of rhetoric.

By the end of the 1960s, however, many people in the United States were skeptical of abstract truths spoken from on high down to the people below in concrete situations that were challenging and in need of good news. This led to the collapse of the legitimacy of the United States as authorities—be they presidents, politicians, or pastors—were no longer bestowed

---

25. Randolph, *Renewal*, 17.
26. Randolph, *Renewal*, 19.
27. Randolph, *Renewal*, 19.
28. Craddock, *Authority*, 26.

with unquestioned authority. This was an age of protest and revolution against unquestioned authority. For Craddock, the preacher in the pulpit was out of touch with the reality experienced by younger generations. The preacher remained behind stained glass windows, looking out on the world rather than working in the world or letting the concerns of the times shape the sermon behind the stained glass.

Craddock lamented how even the way church buildings were designed exacerbated the problem, as the preacher looks down from on high as the expert, and the people look up toward the expert for information.[29] Craddock said this form (technology! Artifact!) distances people from the life-giving word of God. A New Homiletic approach could breathe life back into the sermon and the people back into the story of God. Initially published in 1971, Craddock's *As One Without Authority* midwifed a new approach to sermon design, informed by a turn to the listener.[30]

Practitioners of the New Homiletic introduced a proposal for the sermon's *how* that took seriously the world of the Bible and the world of human beings breathing and experiencing the sermon each Sunday in creative tension. Craddock said, "Taking the congregation out of context is as much a violation of the Word of God as taking the scripture out of context."[31] Sermon preparation then involves more than studying the sacred text. It involves pastoral care, reading the news and novels, and listening to the stories around us to bring them into God's story.

Additionally, the New Homiletic invited new forms of preaching shaped by the medium of the gospel story and the storytelling media of the day.[32] In the next wave of New Homiletics in the 1980s, Eugene Lowry and his "Loop" in *The Homiletical Plot* played with the movement of the twenty-minute sitcom for the sermon form, plotting movement from itch to scratch in the experience of the listener, from *oops* and *ugh* about real

---

29. Craddock, *Authority*, 15.

30. Some have argued that Craddock's dialogical "New Homiletic "is nothing new at all for preaching,particularly in the black church. See, for example, Andrews, "New to Whom?" Andrews states that the practice of turning to the listener, central to Craddock and the New Homiletic, was not new to oral and folk cultures of communication organic to African cultures.

31. Craddock, *Authority*, 104.

32. Again, my mentor and advisor, the late Dale P. Andrews, challenged the notion that the New Homiletic, with its emphasis on inductive logic and storytelling, was new to *all* preaching communities. African, Asian, indigenous, feminist, and womanist communities had been centering nonlinear, nondeductive, narrative communication for generations.

situations in need of resolution to *whee!* and *yeah!* as the gospel reshapes what seemed unsolvable. David Buttrick interacted with film studies in his *Homiletic* and encouraged preachers to plan a sermon not with points (three points and a poem!) but with a plot (moves and structures).

NEW HOMILETICS AND THE DANGER OF A SINGLE STORY

Much of Craddock's work emphasized the imagination of the pastor to bring the sermon to its storied life. Other homiletics scholars questioned whether a preacher could really be inclusive of others' stories without intentional, consistent, and programmed structures for *listening* to perspectives within and beyond their congregation. Roundtable discussions of the mid- to late 1990s began to offer tangible methods for bringing in other voices without relying solely on pastoral imagination. John S. McClure's *Roundtable Pulpit* and Lucy Atkinson Rose's *Sharing the Word* seem to be the future of preaching Clyde Reid hoped for decades before—taking collaboration and conversation seriously.

What is postmodernism, exactly? John D. Caputo, in his book, *Philosophy and Theology*, defines the postmodern ethos as "minutely close attention to detail, a sense for the complexity and multiplicity of things, for close readings, for detailed histories, for sensitivity to differences."[33] Both McClure and Rose imagine and implement preaching preparation that is dialogical and postmodern in approach in order to discover complexity and bring it into the preaching event.

McClure, heavily influenced by the work of Emmanuel Levinas, calls for preaching that resists the tendencies of "Sovereign preaching." When you look at the list below, you will see how similar it is to aspects of print technoculture that formed a particular homilecclesiology critiqued by Reid earlier. Sovereign modes of preaching, according to McClure:[34]

1. tend to deny relevance of hearer's experience.
2. tend to "preclude communal interpretation of the Word" since the preacher has a direct line.
3. tend to use an assertive rhetoric that turns coercive.
4. tend to set God's word as fixed and unchanging in changing contexts.

33. Caputo, *Philosophy*, 50.
34. McClure, *Roundtable*, 31ff.

Note again how the list above is markedly similar to aspects of print technoculture that formed a particular homilecclesiology critiqued by Reid earlier!

Impacted by Levinas's ethic of the "other," McClure proposed preaching that grows out of an *encounter* with others—meaning those human strangers inside and outside of the church who also represent the Holy Other. This engagement renders the gospel a public gospel, one discovered only through a journey together in the public realm. Truth emerges only in real—not imagined—face-to-face encounters, rather than rooted in the preacher's mind, waiting to be transmitted to and received by a passive audience. McClure's methodology pursues "nutritive empowerment, or power *for* others" rather than power over others.[35] By strategically meeting face-to-face every week as a church to discuss the text for worship, "*interactive forms of persuasion*," rather than coercive forms, emerge.[36] Power is shared as the message is shaped by an expanding number of voices, rather than the preacher's voice alone.

McClure calls for boundaries between preacher and congregation, though not in the sovereign sense of gap/distance. True to Levinas, there is fundamental beloved strangeness that prevents the preacher and people from knowing one another fully. Difference is the accent that keeps the conversation going and preaching open-ended.[37] Thus, the sermon, our effort to bring forth the living Word in the preaching ministry, is not over when the preacher leaves the pulpit. Rather, it is only another beginning in which the Word can emerge through the lives of the community hearing and participating in the preaching ministry. Ultimately, McClure's method aspires not to a "fusing of horizons" or a "like-minded" or "tolerant" church but a "*learning* community of deeply engaged strangers."[38]

It is important to note that for McClure collaborative preaching does not pursue equality and mutuality, because it cannot. Conversation is always in a state of inequality or "asymmetry," though the balance must shift, McClure argues, so that one partner does not always hold more power over the direction of the conversation.[39] The challenge to leaders, then, is to en-

---

35. McClure, *Roundtable*, 20.
36. McClure, *Roundtable*, 20.
37. McClure, *Roundtable*, 53.
38. McClure, *Roundtable*, 54.
39. McClure, *Roundtable*, 52.

sure the asymmetry is not habitually over and against those at—or not yet at—the table.

Beginning with an image of a church-shaped pulpit, Lucy Rose takes the collaborative preaching of McClure one step further by attending to the beloved community in its struggle to be followers and *preachers* of the word. She insists on a need for more radical, egalitarian forms of conversational preaching among the community, but she ends her project with a proposal and a question of *how* this preaching occurs, rather than a one-size-fits-all model to pursue.

While "strangeness" and "otherness" are at the core of McClure's collaborative preaching, Rose pursues instead the image of "cohort" for the relationship between preachers and people. Connectedness, not sacred distance, is the aim of Rose's conversational preaching. Rose understands the distance between pulpit and pew to be a by-product of modern Western male sovereign models of preaching, in which the underlying "assumption seems to be that the preacher and the congregation are different because of the preacher's superior understanding of truth or the gospel, interpretation of scripture, of faith experience, which—being more biblical, more theologically sound, or perhaps simply more faithful—should be transferred to the congregation."[40] (Note again the resonances between this assumption and print technoculture and its hierarchies of knowledge that put institutional forms of education above local, oral knowledge and wisdom.)

Rose believed that a conversational ethos for preaching is powerful enough to upset the balance of power by surrounding the pulpit, "traditionally the source of power," with preaching and power and authority that is shared.[41] This ethos cultivated over time by conversational preaching traits should organically lead "those who are ordained to resist monopolizing the pulpit" and to instead "reenvision their role as ensuring that preaching"—that is the conversation of the congregational cohort that takes place all week long—"occurs."[42] She also claimed that cultivating conversational preaching would give way to a nonhierarchical context in which "the term preacher" is no longer "a synonym for one who is ordained or for the minister who controls access to the pulpit" but is a term for all people.[43] In

---

40. Rose, *Sharing*, 128.
41. Rose, *Sharing*, 123.
42. Rose, *Sharing*, 123.
43. Rose, *Sharing*, 123.

other words, we could become not only a church that is a priesthood of all believers, but one that is a preaching hood of all believers as well.

Before the birth of Google, McClure and Rose pushed homiletics toward concrete practices for bringing more voices around the preachers' desk as she designed the sermon on Sunday. These practices allowed for more complexity to emerge as the preacher prepared for the Sunday preaching event. Stories were encouraged. And not canned stories from a printed book of sermon illustrations (no offense to *Chicken Soup for the Soul*). Real stories gathered in a particular context around Scripture. The preacher was tasked with honoring and sharing these stories in the sermon. No longer would the pastor's experience be the only one contributing to the proclamation. Feedforward and feedback become part of the preaching ministry. Each does Reid and Howe proud by tackling the monological illusion in ways graspable for the church as it exists in the North American mainline today.

However, the preacher is still the preacher. The preacher still stands in the place of authority to deliver the message. The preacher is responsible for weaving, synthesizing, and delivering multiple messages at the roundtable for one and all. If the pastor is a cis white man, he is attempting to honor the testimony of a queer Puerto Rican woman to the best of his ability. A worthy task, but one that takes great care. McClure and Rose name the caution and humility required of preachers as they do their best to tell other people's stories, like a game of telephone. Try as we might, a preacher cannot imitate the incarnation of the original testimony shared by another human. The preacher's voice, tone, and presence are the medium of the monological message, dressed up conversationally, no matter how hard preachers may try to go through erasure to allow others to be known and encountered in all their differences.

The New Homiletic dealt with issues of power and authority by shifting sermonic forms from deductive-rhetorical-logic-driven preaching to inductive-story-theological-driven preaching. Craddock and others in the New Homiletic, including Rose and McClure, operate under the assumption that the pulpit-pew method of preaching, from one messenger to many receivers, is a solid foundation, though one in need of a bit of renovation. With enough listening and pastoral attention to people around them, preachers could amplify the many stories over time in their voice without losing the perspective of others.

Can a monological sermon decenter the preacher's perspective, voice, and authority for others to contribute? Can a monologue ever fully allow for "contra-diction" as McClure describes it, the gathering of a community of real bodies—even nonhuman bodies in crisis—with all their multiplicity and range of beliefs, experiences, and interpretations about holy things? Perhaps it is time to really question the how of preaching—from being the work on the paid pastor to the shared ministry of midwifing the word into flesh.

Buzz, buzz, buzz. Something is shifting.

THE NEW HOMILETIC IN A NEW MEDIA ERA: IMAGINING WHAT COULD BE

In 2011, Ronald Allen, a process theology homiletician, revisited his 1991 "Agendae for Homiletics" and pondered before the Academy of Homiletics about the future of preaching as new technologies and shifts encounter the discipline. Allen explicitly asks, "how far can the boundary of the notion of preaching extend" and so "prompt us to reconfigure our understandings of the norms for what counts as preaching, expressions of preaching, who can preach, etc.?"[44] Allen lamented that while homileticians have succeeded in presenting a diversity of sermonic forms in the postmodern era, they have yet to dive deeper into what the emerging "postmodern ethos" could mean for *how* we preach and *who* gets to preach.[45]

The New Homiletic dealt with issues of power and authority by shifting sermonic forms from deductive, modern logic-driven preaching to inductive, story-driven preaching. However, Craddock and others in the New Homiletic imply in their *how* that one-way, sender-receiver preaching is the most effective mode of incarnational communication. Reid's challenge goes unanswered, though the contributions of Rose and McClure did bring some of his suggestions for dialogical preaching into practice.

As Allen suggests, it may be time to allow a new *how* for preaching to be informed by the Gadfly of our network, social media, TikTok, technoculture that subverts single stories. But now, this may also require a new *who* for preaching.

Before the chapter ends, it is important to shift away from a primarily homiletics-preacher perspective and mention the perspective of

44. Allen, "Issues."
45. Allen, "Issues."

congregants as well. Reader, we cannot take the agency of congregants for granted! They are not empty vessels. Since the beginning, even when preaching became more driven by the ordained, sermon listeners have interacted with the preacher and the Holy Spirit to make meaning pertinent to their situations. The miracle is this takes place even if the preacher did not intend that meaning in their focus and function statements.

As a film studies major in college, part of my training was to listen to the perspectives of people in the audience. My wise professors always reminded us that despite the carefully planned plotline, cinematography, directing, and editing of the collaborators on a film, the audience will not simply receive *the* message of *the* film as if they are passive receptacles of art.

In film, and I would argue also as in preaching, we always already have *Artists in the Audience*. This was one of my course texts in college when I studied film. No matter how much the director, cinematographer, or producer desire for the audience to receive their final product in a particular way, meaning is made in and through the lives of the audience members—their preferences, experiences, social location, etc. We expect to be moved by the art of film, and in a way, we become part of the production team as we immerse ourselves in a film world.

Homileticians Marianne Gaarden and Marlene Ringgaard Lorensen observed this phenomenon of meaning-making in the audience for preaching. They utilized empirical studies to explore how churchgoers in Scandinavia exercise agency within the shared environment of the sanctuary and "create new meaning and understanding."[46] Gaarden and Lorensen interviewed churchgoers about what they did when they listened to sermons. Their findings support the notion that "preaching involves a reciprocal relation" between the preacher and the congregation.[47] Their conclusion is counter to the assumption about agency for the laity under the traditional broadcast framework when they claim that the "churchgoers are to be understood as the primary authors of preaching and that preachers have the role of co-author."[48]

However, the meaning authored in diversity by the people in the pews tends to remain within the mind and heart of each individual. How often

---

46. Gaarden and Lorensen, "Listeners as Authors," 28.
47. Gaarden and Lorensen, "Listeners as Authors, 30.
48. Gaarden and Lorensen, "Listeners as Authors," 31.

outside of coffee hour do we hear each other incarnate the preacher's word in our situations?

Could you imagine the insight we could gain about each other if we turned to our neighbors and really heard what stories are being co-authored in the interaction of Spirit, sermon, and individual? What do we miss out on as a church body when the diverse responses to the single story the preacher proposes from the pulpit aren't being shared? How much stronger might our fellowship be if we began to turn our gaze from the pulpit and to our neighbors instead?

Buzz . . . buzz . . . we are being invited to give it a try.

SUMMARY

This chapter showed examples of thinkers, mostly homileticians, challenging the inherited communication norms from print technoculture. In the early twentieth century, print technoculture evolved into broadcast and mass media, with the tools of radio and television amplifying the norms already embedded in print technoculture. These norms set one speaker expert at a distance from the audience. The techniques for effective communication are based on one-way transmission. Little care is given to the feedback from the audience.

Clyde H. Reid asked whether modern preaching, shaped by print technoculture, has lost effectiveness. Reid critiques the traditional monological approach to preaching, where the preacher delivers a message without much consideration for dialogue or feedback from the congregation. He argues that this approach is outdated and ineffective in engaging listeners and bringing about meaningful change in their lives. Reid suggests that preaching should evolve to incorporate dialogue and interaction with the congregation, drawing inspiration from emerging communication theories. He also challenges the hierarchical structure of traditional preaching, advocating for a more collaborative and inclusive approach where multiple voices contribute to the sermon.

Reid and Howe's perspective aligns with the New Homiletic movement, which emphasizes the importance of understanding the context and experiences of the audience in shaping the sermon. Homileticians have sensed this issue since the 1960s and have worked toward solutions through shifts in sermon content and preparation. The New Homiletic sought to incorporate stories of modern-day ordinary people in dialogue with God's holy stories in Scripture to bridge the gap between preachers and people. Engaging story language and frames, the new homiletic promoted dynamic theological story worlds to immerse the congregation in the hopes that they would leave worship changed or touched by an encounter with God's living word.

Finally, recent scholarship in homiletics through the lenses of laity shows that preachers already have co-authors for their sermons. Human beings are wired for meaning-making, not passive receptacles of information. The communication loop is fragmented when the preacher and neighbors in the congregation aren't prompted to share their interpretations of the activity of God's word and work within. Our current structures, still operating under the monological illusion, do not empower the laity to see themselves as co-authors of the sermon. Unless prompted, we aren't likely to open up to each other about how the sermon takes shape through our lives.

Almost thirty years ago, postmodern contributors to the New Homiletic could not have imagined a culture of communication such as the one we are immersed in today, wherein our smartphones are wired to buzz and beep out an ever-flowing stream of conversation, 24/7. How might this climate reimagine roundtable preaching and churches? McClure offers insight by approaching new media and theology through "mashup" practices in pop music. Recently, McClure invited the reader to conceptualize *doing* (not consuming) theology in similar collaborative and creative ways and offered a case study for approaching the homiletic process.[49] But how is the preaching task radically transformed in this climate of mashups, new media, and the like? In other words, do we need a new media homiletic that engages the Gadfly as it buzzes in our ear?

Chapter 4 will finally offer a more detailed portrait of the technoculture emerging from our new media in a postmodern era. Hold onto your *why*, your curiosity, and your smart device as the Gadfly comes center stage.

CONVERSATION PROMPTS

1. How do you think the lack of dialogue and feedback in traditional preaching impacts the effectiveness of communication?

---

49. See McClure, *Mashup Religion*.

2. Can you identify instances where you've experienced or observed a disconnect between the preached message and the congregation's response?

3. What are some key principles of the New Homiletic movement, and how do they differ from traditional or "sovereign" preaching methods?

4. How might collaborative preaching practices help to create a more inclusive and diverse religious community?

5. What are some potential challenges or limitations of collaborative preaching, and how might they be addressed?

6. How can preachers balance their own perspectives and authority with the need for inclusivity and dialogue in the preaching process?

7. Do you think it's possible for a preacher to fully erase their own perspective and allow for diverse voices to be heard in the sermon? Why or why not?

4

Oh, Shifts! Meeting the Gadfly of This Digital Age

Technology is neither good nor bad; nor is it neutral. —Melvin Kranzberg[1]

Technology can become sacramental, it can become a bearer of the self-giving love of God to a broken world. But in order for this to happen, Christian faith and practice must establish a genuine and ongoing discourse with technologized society. —Susan J. White[2]

IN THIS CHAPTER, WE will finally examine the technoculture of this time in order to engage the Gadfly. I hope you see why it was important to start with the immediate past before moving forward. We are responding to what came before, what became normal in the preaching of the church.

Now, we will discuss answers to questions such as: How can we preach with integrity to a congregation that is both in-person and online? Can these social media tools empower us to preach in ways that align with our *why* for preaching, or should they be avoided?

We are at a watershed moment for preaching. Changes in technology have introduced the pastor to platforms for preaching that allow for novel means of dialogical preaching unimaginable fifty, even fifteen years ago. Changes in technological tools or artifacts relate to changes in how people know, relate, and communicate. As I've said before, scholars suggest that we

1. Kranzberg, "Technology and History," 545.
2. White, *Christian Worship*, 129.

are in the foothills of a drastic culture shift akin to the transition introduced by the printing press over five hundred years ago. Just as a shift from orality to literacy introduced new platforms, structures, and models for preaching in print and mass media technoculture, so will this transition period offer homiletics novelty in the form of tools and patterns for communication.

In the last chapter, we took a brief look into how homiletics, the study of preaching, has been wrestling with the Gadfly's questions about the efficacy of models for preaching that emerged after Gutenberg in a postmodern, pre-Google era. Now, we are turning toward preaching after Google.

When a Gadfly appears, a shift is generally nearby. Rather than resisting change as inherently and essentially bad (sinful, not of God), can we ask with curiosity what is possible, faithful, beautiful, and just amid this change that can help preaching bear more fruit in the lives of participants?

NAVIGATING THE BADLANDS OF DISRUPTIVE INNOVATION

For a moment, we are going to listen to voices beyond the church who have articulated the five-hundred-year shift that we are currently experiencing. It might comfort you that the church is not the only institution navigating these shifts, as Mary O'Hara-Devereaux describes in her book *Navigating the Badlands: Thriving in the Decade of Radical Transformation*.

O'Hara-Devereaux, CEO of Global Foresight and business forecaster and strategist, offers as a guide for participants in the business world hoping to find direction for their work in an emerging technological age. Her metaphor of badlands describes the rugged time between the Industrial Age and the as-yet-to-be-determined full promise of the Information Age. To frame the trajectory of this shift, O'Hara-Devereaux took the *longue durée*, a French phrase that translates to "long duration." This approach looks back over time to see the long, slow accumulation of shifts and changes in history, like Phyllis Tickle and her work *The Great Emergence*, mentioned in chapter 2.

O'Hara-Devereaux and her colleagues looked at changes in technology and culture (technoculture) that emerged with the invention of writing in 3500 BC and on into the end of the 1990s, to forecast the foothills of a new age to be found in 2020. She and her colleagues "settled on the belief that we are now some fifty years into a seventy-five-year historical cycle of disruptive innovation."[3] These seventy-five years of shift are the badlands, an environment known for being precisely what is implied: dry, broken, and void of vegetation. And here we are! We are now sixty-five years into this vastly disruptive cycle of technological innovation.

In rapid succession over the last fifty years, says O'Hara-Devereaux, the world has developed new knowledge and tools in everything from chemistry to physics and biology. Perspectives have shifted, and assumptions have been challenged through these technologies. The twentieth century was a century of innovative technologies: radar, medicine, explosives, laser, television, micro-processing, cloning, and genetic engineering.[4] With each innovation, says O'Hara-Devereaux, economic and social contexts for companies perpetually shift—though inherent with the messiness of the "badlands" is an inability to pinpoint clear cause and effect patterns. The result has been a new world, one our grandparents would never have anticipated.

Okay. Many of us know this. But maybe it helps to be reminded that we've dealt with (oh no, here comes the word . . .) *unprecedented* shifts in our lifetimes. What is most important to note for individuals and institutions during this disruptive era is that decisions made in the thick of it are giving shape to the emerging age. O'Hara-Devereaux states that these disruptive cycles are characterized by messiness, rupture, and monumental institutional changes. These cycles and the waves they set in motion, in turn, shift business and organizational life *to the core*. Not merely on the surface (we have a Twitter, oh sorry, X handle! We have a website!). They impact the why as well as the how of all that humans do and inhabit.

According to O'Hara-Devereaux, systems and institutions can react in two ways, one that leads to survival at best and one that can lead to thriving. The path of survival (at best) and extinction (worst-case scenario) is to hunker down and wait for the season of innovation to slow down and settle so that a clear picture of the situation reveals itself. The path of thriving for institutions to cultivate adaptive strategies now, even without an idea of what the world will look like ten or even five years from now. She argues that those who hunker down will likely find that their identity (their why!) as institutions is forced to break apart, leading either to re-emergence or dissolution. Writing in 2004, she prophetically claimed that those who will

---

3. O'Hara-Devereaux, *Badlands*, 6.
4. O'Hara-Devereaux, *Badlands*, 43.

not make it to the foothills of 2025 (and the age that is to come) avoid risk, stifle diversity, are slow to make decisions, and are addicted to stability.

Whew. Read that line again. I can think of so many of our institutions that have all of those attributes. Not a good sign, unless we can really claim hope and belief in life *after* death as Easter people.

So, what if we choose the adaptive option instead of hunkering down for the foreseeable future? What attributes and practices can lead us to thrive in an age of radical, disruptive innovation? O'Hara-Devereaux helpfully lists attributes found in communities that make it to the foothills of the new age to come. She says that instead of avoiding and stifling diversity, thriving institutions will engage cultures that are different and unlike the dominant culture of the community/organization and learn something new about themselves.

Second, instead of being slow to make decisions, those who thrive will make decisions quickly, not for the sake of putting on the latest fads but out of integrity. This requires organizations to be clear about their mission, purpose, and, you guessed it, their *why* for existing. Third, organizations that thrive into the next age *seek* collisions rather than avoid them. They won't view dissent or conflict as things to be avoided or shut down. Instead, if trained in how to work through conflict, the organization will come out stronger on the other side of awkwardness. Finally, thriving organizations will be fast learners. They will seek input from other experts, take risks, fail, and learn from the failure. In summary, organizations that will emerge as healthy leaders in the age of technoculture to come will seek diversity, know their why, and make quick decisions so long as they don't compromise their purpose, seek conflict and work through it, and be quick learners.

A comfort for the attentive historian, and something O'Hara-Devereaux reminds us of, is that there have been many disruptive cycles, and the world has not ended. The printing press did not erase the Roman Catholic Church, and Google will not erase the many forms of Christianity in existence today. But not all forms will persist. New forms will emerge. Institutions and worldviews have been profoundly impacted in each stormy cycle. Organizations that die become compost for the new. Resurrection happens.

This portrait of navigating the badlands lends itself nicely to the work that remains in the rest of this book around preaching and technology. As anxieties rise, let us not hunker down, avoid, and ignore what is emerging.

Remember our mantra from Kranzberg, whose sage advice opened this chapter: Technology is neither good nor bad nor neutral.

NAMING SOME KEY CULTURAL SHIFTS IN TECHNOCULTURE: 1993–2022

At this point, we will spend some time naming the emerging themes of our present technoculture. As we discussed in chapter 2, *technoculture* is a term that encompasses the reality of how technology and culture reciprocally shape one another. Like all cultures, it can be challenging to define because technoculture is the water we swim in daily. Yet the anxiety, misunderstanding, and rapid changes in our technoculture highlight that we are amid a shift—from the mass media, print technoculture of the modern era into the social media, network technoculture of the postmodern era.

The tools of communication that are staples in our technoculture include smart phones, tablets, smart watches, and the like. These devices presence us on the web. For that reason, we will first look at the development of the web over the last two decades. Then we will look at the shift from personal computers sitting on a desk in a particular space in the home or at work to the smart devices today. The cross-pollination of evolution in these two areas of technoculture then bring us to the platforms developed by Big Tech to capitalize on the new media. The new media—social in nature hence the term "social media"—we engage with these devices emerge from and with our understandings of presence and communication in the age of smartphones and watches in Web 3.0, X (Twitter) or Threads, TikTok, Instagram, Snapchat, Facebook, Bluesky, and other sites, and whatever next month's new social media platform will be shaped by and shape our understandings of communication, community, and presence.

Shift: Web 1.0 to 3.0

When the World Wide Web (hereafter, web) emerged from limited accessibility to a broader audience in the early 1990s, it still carried aspects of broadcast and print technoculture. Most content was read-only and static.[5] However, AOL launched its chat service, Instant Messenger, in 1989. A hint

---

5. Gould, *Gospel*, 4.

Oh, Shifts! Meeting the Gadfly of This Digital Age

of what was to come! As early as 1990, 42 percent of Americans had used a computer.[6]

This first wave of shift, known as Web 1.0, was accelerated by the release of Mosaic 1.0 in 1993. The Mosaic browser enabled the public to explore pockets of the Internet (a grid of global computer networks established in the 1970s) through "surfing the web" to connect to websites. By 1994, "11 million American households [were] equipped to ride the information superhighway."[7] I was in one of those households, and I remember sitting down with my dad to learn about this web (though I was interested primarily in playing Math Blaster and Wheel of Fortune). I can still hear the noise of the modem as he plugged us into the Internet through the phone line. These were the days of "going online" and then "signing off" to re-enter the "real world."

You may be surprised to know how many now household names launched their businesses online in 1995: Amazon, craigslist, Match.com, eBay, and Windows 95's Internet Explorer. While users can surf, purchase books and Pizza Hut food, and send emails during this phase, it is still mainly a read-only web that reflects the one-way transmission of mass media. While some information could be exchanged, the consumer passively interacted with sites rather than making and shaping a personalized online identity.[8] Only a webmaster can update users and manage the content of the website.[9]

Web 1.0 phases into Web 2.0 in 2005 with a shift from read-only into a read-write interaction. Why 2005? Because now the platforms that are still most frequently used today under the umbrella of social media are made public. Web 2.0 introduces platforms that allow people to organize themselves around common interests on the Internet and participate more in content generation.[10] By 2005, 8 percent of adult American Internet users are participating in sports fantasy leagues online.[11] People are donating money to causes online, such as Hurricane Katrina relief organizations, and selling things online. Reddit is founded in 2005 and a new culture of niche online communities enters the scene. YouTube is also founded in this year.

6. Pew Research Center, "World Wide Web Timeline."
7. Pew Research Center, "World Wide Web Timeline."
8. Choudhury, "Web 1.0 to Web 4.0," 8096.
9. Choudhury, "Web 1.0 to Web 4.0," 8096.
10. Choudhury, "Web 1.0 to Web 4.0," 8097.
11. Pew Research Center, "World Wide Web Timeline."

"The Facebook" already entered the scene at Harvard in 2004. And Twitter launches its platform in 2006. Keep in mind this is only (or already) two decades ago! But it's hard for many of us to imagine a world before these standard platforms (as an elderly millennial, I can remember the time before, but my daughters will only ever know this world).

In Web 2.0, the Web is not just a network for information for our consumption; it is a social network. An example of this is the launch of Digg in 2004. Digg users made news social as users voted on whether to "dig up" links to news stories that they like and "bury" the stories they don't like. Blogs, wikis, podcasts, and RSS feeds allow people to create and curate unique online experiences. Communities also become a hallmark of this phase of the social web. Massively multiplayer online role-playing games (MMORPG) such as World of Warcraft and Second Life allow people to create and curate online spaces, avatars, and rubrics for being part of virtual societies.

Currently, most of us dwell in the climate of Web 3.0. The distinction between Web 2.0 and 3.0 is yet to be strongly identified. However, it is interesting to notice how 2016 is the chosen year to mark the beginning of Web 3.0. In the United States, this election year revealed how siloed we'd become from people on the algorithm's "other side" of political affiliation. Because of the echo chambers on each side of the political spectrum, Republicans were just as certain as Democrats that their candidate would win. The algorithms cleaned up contrasting perspectives and created an illusion of unified opinion, especially for Democrats, which were disrupted by the election results. Even news sources like the *New York Times* seemed stunned by the results. We will talk more about this reality later in this chapter. I think the defining characteristic of Web 3.0 is how scholars have grappled with the impact of social media, algorithms, prisms, and fake news on politics and religion. As we will discuss shortly, it is also the time for the most portable devices to engage new media.

But Web 3.0 was also a time of challenge to some early institutions on the web. Snapchat and TikTok ushered in more of a departure from the written (typed) word of Tweets and Facebook posts to the audio/visual world of communication. Stories (Facebook) and Reels (Instagram) were added to Web 2.0 social platforms to meet the demand. Additionally, this age has seen more programs and platforms that work to streamline the social media presence of persons and institutions across all platforms at once (HubSpot or the Meta Suite, for example). New media moguls have also become just that: moguls. Governments around the globe are working to regulate Big Tech and its big influence on society and protect the free market so that monopolies like Meta and X don't get to grow without healthy competition.

Humming in the background of this overview of Web development from 1989 to now is the evolution of devices that allow us to go online to consume, curate, and share content. The greatest change in technoculture from the time of Web 1.0, when online digital media were static and reader-only, generated by fewer people, to now is that the Web has become more user-particular, participatory, and collaborative in nature. This makes these new media distinct from television and radio, some of the last new media of the print technoculture, which delivered read or listen-only content broadly from a few sources and with little chance for participation. As we will discuss later, this has led to shifts in technoculture from consumer to collaborator. Now, we will briefly review thirty years of shifting accessibility to tools.

Shift: Personal Computers to Smartphones

Web development is one thing, and the tools we use to access the web are just as important. When households first had access to the web, they only did through bulky, gray, personal computers (PCs) that weighed a ton, required proximity to an outlet and phone line, and took up most of your desktop. Physically, we had to set aside time and precious phone line space to go online and surf the web. Socially, there was one computer per household at most. Even schools had computer labs where individuals would go to use a computer. Going online took place in shared spaces.

Log off the line, step away from your desk, and the Internet went on without you. Step outside, and no one could get a hold of you unless you had a beeper, the rare car phone (my dad did!), or a Zack Morris from *Saved by the Bell* mobile phone (presumably a Motorola DynaTAC, according to Google). Sigh. Sounds nice! In 1999, the BlackBerry entered the market and became ubiquitous in business. Mobile or cellular phones were now becoming smartphones with operation systems that allowed for much more than making a phone call. BlackBerry's 2003 6210 integrated a phone with fully functioning email and web browsing. This is the first wave of Web 2.0 and the conclusion of a relationship with the Internet that revolved around a stationary desktop PC from which to log on and log off.

With Web 2.0, our access started to become more portable. Web 2.0 started in 2005, and coincidentally, in the United States, laptops first outsold desktop computers in May 2005.[12] In 2007, the iPhone debuted, and the first Android phone followed in 2008. Do you remember life before texts? While Short Message Service (SMS) text was sent in 1992,[13] texting did not go mainstream until 2000, as cell phones followed BlackBerry and Nokia to include keyboards and the technology for texting to occur across different platforms developed in 1999. Into the 2010s, influenced by the innovation of the iPhone, keyboards were replaced by touchscreen technology. In the first survey conducted by Pew Research in 2011, only 35 percent of Americans owned a smartphone.[14] Cameras continued to improve, capturing higher quality video as well, and new social media platforms emerged to coincide with the technology (Instagram and Snapchat, for example). The quality of the screen continues to improve as well, making our phones another outlet for streaming shows, movies, or gaming (and making our own shorts and games).

Today as I write this in 2024 thirty years after the Web became more accessible to homes across America thanks to PCs and Mosaic 1.0, 15 percent of adults in the United States access the Internet by "smartphone-only."[15] This means a growing number of Americans do not have a PC or laptop for internet access, only their smartphone. Pew Research also indicates that in early 2024, 97 percent of Americans own a cell phone, and 9/10 are smartphone users.[16] Most Americans carry a portal into an ever-growing array of social media platforms in their pockets or on their wrists. And they use them. Constantly.

Now, we will explore how these shifts in technoculture—both around the web and our tools for accessing the web—have also shifted how we

12. Arthur, "Laptops."
13. *Vodafone*, "25 Years."
14. *Vodafone*, "25 Years."
15. Pew Research Center, "Mobile Fact Sheet."
16. There is a slight distinction between smartphone and cell phone and the lines grow fuzzier every year. Both are mobile devices, handheld, able to be used for calls, short message service (SMS), and multimedia message (MMS). These days, most cell phones also have the capacity to go online. A smartphone is the merger of the cell phone with the PDA or personal digital assistant. The PDA tended to require a stylus or pen for input but did not have phone capacity. The smartphone does what the cell can do while also having the capacity to store music, images, and programs. See Pew Research Center, "Mobile Fact Sheet."

view authority, power, relationships, and conversation. These shifts matter because the church's definitions of authority, power, and relationship are still heavily influenced by theology after Gutenberg, as discussed in the previous chapter. The role of the preacher after Gutenberg was to be the authority on the interpretation of the word of God printed in Scripture and explained in textbooks, and the role of the people was to trust and receive his message. Now, after Google, untraditional authorities and influencers inhabit the social network, sharing theological, personal, and philosophical advice with or without traditional grantees of authority. How will "theology after Google" impact the ministry of proclamation? Let's explore together through the following five themes:

1. Changing Understanding of Relational Presence and Place: X-reality
2. A Shift from Consumer to Curator and Collaborator
3. Polarization: Algorithmic Echo Chambers
4. Ambiguous Authorities: Democratization of News and Information
5. Moving at the Speed of the Feed: Time and the Social Media

Each shift offers challenges to and opportunities for the ministry of proclamation today. We know, thanks to Kranzberg, that these tools and cultural situations are not bad, good, or neutral. We need to practice discernment in order to shape the body of Christ through new media and for a world shaped by new media with justice and shalom as our aim.

WRESTLING WITH CULTURAL SHIFTS IN THE AGE OF SMART DEVICES AND WEB 3.0 FOR PREACHING

> What if, instead of seeing the real vs. virtual divide in terms of embodied vs. disembodied we think about the new permutations of digital and virtual technology informing our lives as particular ways we are embodied?[17] —Kathryn Reklis, "X-Reality and the Incarnation"

---

17. Reklis, "X-Reality."

1. Changing Understanding of Relational Presence and Place: X-Reality

There is no solid line between virtual worlds and real worlds anymore. Kathryn Reklis and other scholars of our newest media "describe this disappearing gap as X-reality—reality that moves fluidly across the virtual to real spectrum and wherein virtual or digital space is just a differently mediated way of being real."[18] That is, our whole reality is a blend of face-to-face and face-to-screen-to-screen-to-face engagement. The weave of both is really real to us, an embodied reality that contributes to our becoming. As Christians, we need to move beyond trying to separate out these realities and instead encourage disciples into living faithfully within X-reality.

Three decades ago, going online was an intentional event. We had to dial up a modem and wait for a connection to get to the Internet. Typically, we had to sit at a desktop computer to go online and enter the virtual community. Early on, this led to a framework in which some described the Internet as a virtual or fake world compared to the real world offline. Related are the two contrasting approaches to technology we mentioned earlier in chapter 2: technophobia and technophilia. Both could lean to their extreme presentations of their preference (bias) and suggest that one reality is a better/truer or worse/false/fake reality. This form of argument fits into the classical binary, also known as either/or thinking. Binary thinking does not fit well into postmodern X-reality. Approaching technoculture from the binary theologically, Christians may argue that virtual presence is not real presence. Some may even call it sinful or evil.[19]

But the experience of Web 3.0 resists binary thinking. Try to keep track of how often you experience people's presence through your phone, watch, or computer throughout your day. With every buzz and chime from your phone, you get notifications from social media. With the movement of a finger or two, we respond and react to the presence of a friend on the other end of our device. Then, we seamlessly shift our focus to whatever else we were doing before. We do not have to sit and wait to go online and then sit for a prolonged event to log off—as you can see from the overview of evolution from Web 1.0 to 3.0 and from personal desktop computers to smartphones that connect us to the Internet anytime and anywhere.

---

18. Reklis, "X-Reality." See also Coleman, *Hello Avatar*.
19. I've written on these debates in previously: see Sigmon, "Failure to Discern."

Oh, Shifts! Meeting the Gadfly of This Digital Age

Process theologian and computer consultant Jennifer Cobb, writing in 1998, links a process understanding of God as the Supremely Related One and cyberspace. In *CyberGrace: The Search for God in the Digital World*, Cobb deconstructs the mind/body binary schema to construct a view of virtual reality, an evolving place of process and connection, years before the social media of Web 2.0 and 3.0.[20] This space, according to Cobb, transcends both the mind/body and divisions between the world of the spirit and the world of the machine. She celebrates cyberspace as a place where the Divine may be encountered, and spirituality deepened in the emergence of complexity in that place. We may really encounter someone or something in this graced cyberspace, but how do we evaluate the quality of that meeting?

In Web 3.0 technoculture, face-to-face encounters are not the only real encounters that we have. Thus, according to Reklis, "The work of evaluating whether or not a human connection is real or whether a human interaction is good requires more than assessing if it is virtually mediated or not."[21] In a world where friends "hang out" via Google video service or have whole friend networks based on the internal communications in *World of Warcraft*, the potentials for deep and intimate connection through these platforms are displayed. "If it is the human spirit animating the connections we experience [online]," argues Daniella Zsupan-Jerome in *Connected Toward Communion: The Church and Social Communication in the Digital Age*, "then these connections can and do convey our presence and invite us into a relational, communal experience online."[22]

The dichotomy of virtual vs. real is disrupted in an emerging blended technoculture, but we have not fully transitioned into an ordinary blended reality. Pastors and congregations know this well. For one, anyone who lives in a rural community is aware of how inconsistent and slow Internet connections still are a quarter of the way through the twenty-first century. Additionally, thanks to technological developments in the biomedical field, people live longer than ever.[23] As a result, our churches are experiencing unprecedented multigenerational presence. Preachers must walk the fine line between engaging in the technoculture in ways that connect to younger

---

20. See Cobb, *CyberGrace*.
21. Reklis, "X-Reality."
22. Zsupan-Jerome, *Connected*, 102.
23. Although this notion seems to be changing in the United States. See Centers for Disease Control and Prevention, "Life Expectancy."

generations without leaving our oldest generations behind. Discernment is required to inhabit X-reality well and with mission alignment.

Another tension that comes up again and again in my work as a preaching professor and consultant is the struggle to feel connected as a preacher in a hybrid worship context. *How do I split my attention between the congregation in front of me and the one that may or may not be on the livestream? How can I connect the online community with the community in the building?* These concerns speak to a reasonable desire for preaching: that, like the New Homiletic, it speaks concretely to the listeners, that it responds to visual feedback from the pews, and that it helps strengthen relationships within the congregation. We will talk more about models for preaching that aim toward these desires in the following chapters. However, these concerns do not label people online, at home, or wherever, and streaming worship as fake congregants while those in the building are real. We are moving beyond the binary into X-reality!

Many of us are almost always "online," even in person. For better or worse, this is the nature of an emerging X-reality. These connections feel like real connections to people for many. They are not parsed out as virtual and, therefore, less than real. Binary thinking leads to either/or thinking, leading to this setup: we do this aspect of ministry online or in person, and never shall the two meet. The concept of X-reality helps the pastor and congregation realize that we are not choosing between doing conventional preaching and worshiping in a church with a pulpit and pews or doing these practices online.

But something interesting is buzzing in this X-reality and hybridity: our in-person preaching arrangement is very much the product of modern, print technoculture and Protestant reformation that centered the sermon and seated the audience so that they could best receive the sermon from the authority in the pulpit. Web 3.0 is not arranged in the same way. How does it feel then to embody the passive reception of modern preaching in platforms that enable instant feedback, response, curation, and sharing? Let's look at this key technocultural shift more closely.

2. A Shift from Consumer to Curator and Collaborator

Mass media—newspaper, radio, and television—dominated technoculture of the nineteenth and twentieth centuries. The masses consumed the media and information created, produced, and delivered by a select few. This trend maintained prominence through the 1980s and nineties. Academics like Neil Postman lamented the impact of mass media, particularly television, for its corrosive effects on the brain and society in general (see? There's nothing new under the sun . . . even writing as a new technology was said to be criticized by Socrates in Plato's *Phaedrus*).[24] In the mass media age, recreational activities for many in the United States involved watching sitcoms on the night they aired (nothing to record here unless you had the VCR for it), nightly news, movies, and reading the morning paper. As we saw in the previous chapter, rather than resisting this shift in technoculture, homileticians like Eugene Lowry created a narrative method of structuring sermons out of it in his classic *The Homiletical Plot*. In this sermon method, preachers are encouraged to follow the sitcom's plot trajectory in sermon design in order to engage the listener who has accommodated to this new media. Willow Creek and other megachurches of the 1980s and nineties flourished in this technoculture of mass media entertainment and the show business of keeping consumers entertained. Christians and seekers accustomed to consuming the nightly news from an authority on the television screen found little dissonance with consuming professionally "produced" worship and preaching.

Participation (the sort that Clyde Reid would describe as leading to a complete communication loop) was not easy to cultivate in this era of technoculture. It wasn't designed for the participation of the many, but for efficiently sharing a message with many from one or two leaders. To create and collaborate with the mass media, you could become a journalist or a dedicated author of letters to the editor. To create media, you made short films with a clunky video camera and shared the VHS with a relatively limited group of contacts (I totally did this with friends in high school). There was a glass ceiling for the average citizen wishing to create media.

But then came those shifts in the web and in technology from 1989 to now. And how interesting it is that in this time of shifts, Christian movements like Emergence/Emergent/Fresh Expressions also grew as an antidote to megachurches and their mass-mediated preaching and worship. Emerging churches rummaged through the church's history and reimagined rituals to increase a holistic, multimedia sense of participation in worship and in some instances, such as dinner church expressions, to share the task of preaching with more than just an ordained expert.

---

24. Postman, *Amusing Ourselves to Death*.

By the 2000s, scholars had noticed a generational shift from consumerist postures to participatory postures with media.[25] After years of American free time being filled with television consumption, generations after Gen X watch less television than their parents.[26] When they watch television, they tend to multitask the experience, tweeting and chatting throughout it rather than silently digesting the media offered to them. These are not all simply distracted and shallow youth of the Internet culture, as Nicholas Carr would cast them to be in his book *The Shallows: What the Internet is Doing to Our Brains*.[27] Millennial, Gen Z, and Gen A folks desire more than passive media consumption. How might that change the way we design preaching?

When traditional preaching design is informed by mass media technoculture, all authority and power is given unchallenged to the ones who get to produce information for our consumption. For preachers and pastors, these consumers of technoculture—most notably Boomers—transitioned their gaze from the TV screen to the overhead screen or pulpit without much dissonance. Today, we worry about the presence of teens and young adults looking down at their phones as we speak from the pulpit. As binary thinkers, we may assume that those people are not correctly consuming our message, hence the duress. We may assume they do not have the attention spans to sit back and listen and so, we assume, they learn nothing and aren't fully present in the sermon. But if we shift into the posture of the current technoculture and reexamine authority, power, and community from X-reality in Web 3.0, we see something else taking place, something more interactive and relational.

Even in the early days of social media, studies reveal that most sermon listeners engage in sporadic listening. Congregants drift in and out of focus during a monologue sermon.[28] How could a smartphone help keep the congregant engaged instead of drifting? If X-reality were embraced as a way of participating in your sermon, it might be that the girl in the pew could move beyond the pure consumption of your sermon. Perhaps she will broadcast a portion of your sermon live on Instagram. Maybe she will listen intently for what she thinks are the golden moments of your sermon in two

---

25. See, for example, Jenkins et al., *Confronting the Challenges*; also, McClure, *Mash-up Religion*.

26. Shirky, *Cognitive*, 11.

27. See Carr, *Shallows*.

28. McClure, "Practice of Sermon Listening."

Oh, Shifts! Meeting the Gadfly of This Digital Age

hundred characters or less and share it on X or Threads. Perhaps she will intentionally amplify your message and the gospel of Jesus Christ beyond the limits of the four walls of your sanctuary by creating a TikTok. Perhaps curation and collaboration are more helpful ways for her to digest the message and for the message to become incarnate in the world—through active listening and collaboration.

According to new media scholar Clay Shirky, sharing, curating, and collaborating intentionally with specific groups of people is precisely what anchors community in our technoculture.[29] Consuming tweets and status updates as a lurker does *not* create community. Instead, the more a person engages with social media, the more she feels a genuine part of the community conversation. In X-reality, this is the equivalent of quality face time. To be seen is to be shared. To be heard is to be followed, liked, re-tweeted, and tagged. This is a vital part of our ministry of presence in the current technoculture, just as vital as our presence at coffee hour and fellowship meals. "In a participatory culture," American media scholar Henry Jenkins claims, "members also believe that their contributions matter and feel some degree of social connection with one another."[30] To comment on a post, to answer a question on the sermon in a Tweet, is telling a congregant they are of value to the church, the body of Christ.

As we will discuss in the following key theme, authorities are created in social media by the extent to which participants in technoculture gather around them and interact. Some authorities are very much connected to a persona or face. Others are not. Sometimes, ideas, movements, and hashtags become a faceless authority presence. In this environment, authorities can also come and go while the message remains and is sustained according to how many "converged around the information."[31] Messages themselves can become an authority in this way, without the force of the one who started it. As soon as a tweet is shared, note how quickly people like and/or re-tweet their message.

Although power is potentially democratized in this technoculture, there are still people with more power and amplification of voice on the web than others. Celebrity is a powerful force in social media. In Web 3.0, celebrities can be labeled as influencers and then given more power by platforms to reach a wider audience. Algorithms exist to promote the "most

---

29. Shirky, *Cognitive*, 25.
30. Jenkins et al., *Confronting*, xi.
31. Zsupan-Jerome, *Connected*, 7.

popular and most connected person or idea" and not necessarily the best content, per se.³² The momentum in the network enables those who are in power to accumulate more power and reach in a quantitative measure. However, this power of presence is indeed a result of the collaboration and curation of others who choose to follow particular people and agencies, as well as algorithms in social media that notice "trending" persons and ideas. It becomes a chicken/egg origin story. Once again, traditional one-way conceptions of power and authority do not fit neatly with culture as we find it today.

In sum, new media scholars agree that the technoculture of social media is defined by participation, curation, collaboration, and sharing. Consumerism is not a defining activity of the new social media. Listeners today, generations born into our churches, and the generations we fear losing seek collaboration. They live-tweet the messages they hear. They will grab and remix the messages they hear without asking permission from TikTok. A common hashtag can be the means for a common community to develop and continue to converse around the pastor's preaching, including members of the local church and beyond.

For better or worse (meaning no matter how well, under-, or misinformed they may be), citizens of this culture want to participate in communication and the dissemination of information. Whether they do this with their own voice or by serving as puppets for other dominating voices in the landscape is another matter. But there is a longing to participate that rises to the surface.

3. Polarization: Algorithmic Echo Chambers

Many claim 2016 is the year Web 3.0 phased in. This year revealed the accumulated impact of the algorithms created by social media to keep people liking, scrolling, and sharing. Headlines grappled with "the filter bubble" and "echo chambers" that allowed so many Democrats to not see a Trump victory coming.³³ Drowning in a sea of likeness, our feeds funneled us into silos of political preferences and eroded opportunities to "see" and "share" posts and tweets from friends or public figures that the algorithm deemed "on the other side of us." The hyper-personalization of Web 3.0 and personal smartphones contributed to the construction of a feedback loop of constant

---

32. van Dijck, *Connectivity*, 157.
33. See, for examples, Baer, "'Filter Bubble,'" and El-Bermawy, "Destroying Democracy."

Oh, Shifts! Meeting the Gadfly of This Digital Age

self-affirmation. But what do we lose without the conflict and awkwardness of conversations with people who think and see differently than we do?

Developers attempted to reverse the silo-ing. In 2017, I had students download the Chrome extension FlipFeed for Twitter (as it was then named) and PolitEcho for Facebook. PolitEcho analyzes your Facebook friends and newsfeed to visually demonstrate how the algorithm has filtered what you see in the feed based on what it assumes about your political beliefs. In my case, I saw that while my thousand-plus friends on Facebook represented diverse views on the political spectrum, my feed was catering to my bias (left-leaning) to only show me what friends with the same bias are doing in life. These "political ratings are based on the political Facebook pages" liked.[34] Students were just as confounded by this sorting as we shared our results. Unfortunately, changes to Facebook caused PolitEcho to stop working at a time when we could still benefit from this project.[35]

FlipFeed was created by MIT's Laboratory for Social Machines in order to pull back the veil on Twitter's algorithmic sorting.[36] By adding the Chrome extension, users would find a "flip my feed" button on the left side of the screen under their profile picture to see outside their bubble. When we clicked on the button, we were shown feeds that the algorithm deemed to have opposing views to our own. So, if you are programmed as being right-leaning, the feed flips to show left-leaning posts, and vice versa. I had my students search for a topical hashtag in their normal profile and then under the flipped feed. In real time, we could observe how the same event or topic had different opinions and interpretations amplified by algorithmic sorting. We reflected on the trouble such bubbles create, especially in our ministry, especially if we are citing stories amplified on one side of the political spectrum without awareness of what folks in the pews who may be on the other side are reading in their feeds.

The Laboratory for Social Machines understands technology's non-neutrality and that it is not inherently bad. Using its skills, it works to reverse social media's harmful designs and promote helpful ones. The church could certainly learn from its problem-solving as we seek to engage the Gadfly ourselves!

This polarization based on personalized feedback loops also seems to promote the notion that connection (over likeness) is more valuable than

---

34. *PolitEcho*, "Is Your News Feed a Bubble?"
35. *PolitEcho*, "Is Your News Feed a Bubble?"
36. Bell, "Chrome Extension Fixes."

conversation (through difference). In *Alone Together*, Sherry Turkle, sociologist and founding director of MIT Initiative on Technology and Self, argues that our smart machines, which promote hyper-connection, are slowly detaching us from one another in real time. As we pursue hyper-connection on the Web, Americans become "increasingly insecure, isolated, and lonely."[37] The human voice and face are masked by these ambiguous identities, making it easier to ignore people on one hand and troll or harass them on the other. Dehumanized by our devices, it has become easier to be cruel and vulnerable to the cruelty of others.

In her later work, *Reclaiming Conversation*, Turkle laments how we allow connection to trump conversation. The deep root of failed conversation is the placelessness and facelessness that the web enables. In other words, we can always be anywhere and elsewhere and struggle to be present to our partners, family, friendships, and educational and work environments. In generations who have only known this technoculture, there is "widespread agreement that there is an empathy gap."[38] Turkle's latest release, *The Empathy Diaries*, continues this conversation about how our technoculture can hamper the development of empathy.

What is the solution to these gaps, bubble, and chambers? Conversation, talk, and relationship. In what ways might our preaching play a role in contributing to conversation by moving beyond a monologue form into a dialogue hosted by a pastor who is equipped to handle the inevitable, holy tension that comes about when multiple perspectives meet?

4. Ambiguous Authorities: Democratization of News and Information

In the 1950s and sixties, Americans got their news from the nightly report (Walter Cronkite and the CBS Evening News) along with morning information in the local newspaper. Throughout the country, there was little diversity of opinion to the information being shared. Citizens consumed the information and then went about their day—only those aspiring to be journalists created the news. In the 1960s, in the age of civil rights and the Vietnam war, marginalized groups attempted to disseminate information that challenged the mass media. Still, on the whole, one could know only as much as the mass media put out for consumption.

37. Turkle, *Alone Together*, 157.
38. Turkle, *Reclaiming Conversation*.

Oh, Shifts! Meeting the Gadfly of This Digital Age

As we saw in the previous point about our shift from a media consumer to a collaborator and curator of media, a fundamental change in this technoculture—in countries that allow it—is the democratization of power regarding who gets to have a voice in the public space. Autocracies like Russia and China know full well how unharnessed new media can quickly create and disseminate information without approval from the hierarchical powers. In Web 3.0, those few voices that once dominated the public news and information space "now finds (or loses) itself in a cacophony of comments, opinion, perspectives" of the many voices sharing, spreading, and creating news.[39] In the United States, nearly anyone with a smartphone or PC or access to a public library can start their blog, broadcast their voice, post their music or art, follow the work of others they respect, and connect. We can Yelp, tweet, and give a status report on whatever happens in our world from our point of view. And we can follow others all over the globe by connecting via social media.

Mass media has truly given way to social media in countries with free speech (and subversively in countries without), which ironically is more of a media for the masses than mass media ever could be. Individuals are welcome to produce, curate, collaborate, and consume information in a global web of hashtags and links that lacks traditional geographic and cultural boundaries. Top-down, single-source media maintained high barriers regarding what news and information are accurate and relevant to society. The monopoly on information perpetuated one-way lines of power that led to the press having control over the consumers of it. Low barriers to spreading and creating news and information mark participatory technoculture. Traditional media, such as newspapers and newscasts, struggle to stay relevant by going online, creating Twitter accounts, and striving for timeliness in disseminating news, which is crucial to this technoculture.

Low barriers are not always liberating. Low barriers to who can make or share news can also create ambiguous authorities. If untrained and unthoughtful people share opinions as fact, then we will struggle with truth in Web 3.0. The open-source, nonhierarchical social media infrastructure means fewer checkpoints for vetting false and misleading information. Network communities fueled by loneliness and hostility can breed quickly. Loneliness and hate are a moneymaker in the social media economy. Entrepreneurs around the globe are quickly creating programming that results in netting the greatest number of clicks rather than publishing authentic

---

39. Zsupan-Jerome, *Connected*, 7.

information. Amid this dynamic, even clickbait *Christian* communities are made.

According to an October 2019 report leaked to *MIT Technology Review* by former Facebook employee Jeff Allen, troll farms infiltrate the platform with their clickbait material, reaching as many as 140 million users in the United States each month. The study looked at troll farms specifically based out of Macedonia and Kosovo. These professional organizations "work in a coordinated fashion to post provocative content, often propaganda, to social networks" through Facebook pages, whether or not a user has even followed any of the troll farm's pages.[40] In the early days of the Facebook platform, individual profiles (once only for students with a .edu email address) could gain presence in a network by increasing the number of friends connected to their page. Today, "Pages is the broadcast distribution product on [the Facebook] network," according to Allen. Individuals and organizations can create pages with unlimited follows and likes. "It is where the 'largest voices' of our communities live."[41] As noted, amid this dynamic, even clickbait Christian communities are made. The disturbing truth, according to Allen, is that Facebook's platform "has given the largest voice in the Christian American community to a handful of bad actors, who, based on their media production practices, have never been to church." The data show that all fifteen of the top pages targeting Christian Americans were run by troll farms. According to Allen, "when combined, the troll farms run the largest Christian American Page on Facebook by 20x."[42]

You see that correctly—the most significant page presence on Facebook *by twenty times* that of its nearest competition is run by faceless opportunists in Macedonia and Kosovo who aren't seeking to form disciples but to profit from followers. This creation and curation of Christian content is not from a church, denomination, pastor, or theologian—but from troll farms based out of the Balkans with no experience of or concern for religion in America. The project has nothing to do with Christian mission or formation and everything to do with easy money through getting the most clicks and content shares. The troll farm pages are anonymous, ambiguous authorities, and the content is scraped and reformatted from other sources in the hopes that it will go viral.

---

40. Hao, "Troll Farms."
41. Allen, "How Communities Are Exploited."
42. Allen, "How Communities Are Exploited."

Oh, Shifts! Meeting the Gadfly of This Digital Age

On the web, countless self-proclaimed theologians are spreading their word to the people. A pastor who wishes to maintain a monopoly on theological knowledge will struggle to accept the democratization of information, including theology, through social media. Today, the fact is that clergy and academics are no longer "the sole communicators of faith."[43] All over social media, "'amateur' voices of authentic faith emerge alongside, and blog, tweet, post, create, and share in the digital context."[44] For this reason, we need to make faithful disciples for the technoculture, who can communicate their beliefs, who can discern the authenticity and truth in the claims of other amateur theologians, and who are not swayed by just any theological know-it-all tweeting out the gospel of Jesus. The homilecclesiology I propose in the following chapters seeks to empower the church to do just that.

According to professor of communications Peter Horsfield, "authority ascribed in digital practice is one earned in the process of interaction on specific topics or issues, a type of authority that is more common in oral-dominant communities than in the aloof, institution-based authority that most churches have carried into this third millennium."[45] This quote highlights how authority is given in Web 3.0 through practices that blend the previous shift (to curation and collaboration) and the next shift (timely communication). Authorities emerge in social media as they stay in dialogue with situations unfolding in our feeds and interact with other curators and the people commenting on their posts. Authority is not necessarily granted with a title or a link to a well-known institution. Institutions that do not move at the pace of dialogue, and here Horsfield is calling out the church specifically, come off as aloof. This brings us to the fifth and final shift: time.

5. Moving at the Speed of the Feed: Time and the Social Media

A change for those steeped in the slow, careful, cautious print age technoculture is the rapid pace at which news stories hit the public, gain traction, and are replaced with the next breaking event in the social media technoculture. Authorities in social media are those who are most often re-tweeted, re-posted, and interacted with. They are those who can comment

---

43. Zsupan-Jerome, *Connected*, 91.
44. Zsupan-Jerome, *Connected*, 91.
45. Horsfield, *From Jesus to the Internet*, 266.

on a breaking event in the immediate moment. Authorities commenting on events that occur even a day ago are likely to be overlooked or ignored. Thus, Horsfield claims, the most important messages are not those that reveal prolonged pondering and depth; they are instead messages posted in a timely, immediate fashion.[46]

This is an example of how the tools change expectations. Smartphones and Web 3.0 are artifacts/tools that allow for the many to quickly create and share a perspective of a news event as it happens. Heartbreaking scenes from Palestine disrupt my newsfeed as I write this chapter. At the same time, influencers and so-called authorities in the social media world are critiqued for not commenting on the social crises as they unfold locally and globally.[47] The expectation in this landscape is that influencers will pay attention and comment at the speed of the feed.

We take to social media to hear a word of wisdom, inspiration, or frustration from our chosen authorities. We expect to hear from them sooner rather than later. By the time the nightly news airs, we already know the events of the day and those events that the newscast has not had the time to organize for a clean and produced news story. In Web 3.0, production value matters less than timeliness as an authorizing feature of news. Even the *New York Times* redesigned its web page and adopted a digital-first strategy to maintain its place as a news authority in the digital age.[48]

Another time-related shift that we all need to be aware of is attention span. You are a rare creature nowadays if you've made it this far in the book without stopping to look at your phone, check your Fitbit, or ask Google something. Studies show that one result of the abundance of information at our fingertips and the design of scroll interfaces is a shortened attention span. Our attention span is shortened concerning social media as well as books, television, conversation, and, naturally, preaching. The longitudinal study found that "the accelerating ups and downs of popular content are driven by increasing production and consumption of content, resulting in a more rapid exhaustion of limited attention resources."[49] The research suggests that the exhaustion of attention resources supports the concern raised by Nicholas Carr in 2010: the Internet is spreading our collective attention thin. This research highlights once again the impact of technology

---

46. Horsfield, *From Jesus to the Internet*, 265.
47. See Spiers, "I Don't Have to Post."
48. *The New York Times*, "Our Strategy."
49. Lorenz-Spreen et al., "Accelerating Dynamics."

on culture, including our biology and psychology! As Carr says in *The Shallows*, "With the exception of alphabets and number systems, the Net may well be the single most powerful mind-altering technology that has ever come into general use. At the very least, it's the most powerful that has come along since the book."[50]

According to Carr's research, the page deepened our attention span (no wonder people listened to hours-long sermons in the seventeenth and eighteenth centuries), but Web 3.0 has cut it down. What's a preacher to do? One solution that will be part of the new media homiletic in the following chapters is conversation and collaboration sustained over time to help cultivate and sustain attention on topics vital to the church.

Another theme emerging with this technoculture regarding time is asynchronous interaction. People interact with one another on new media platforms at their own pace. The gathering is not always "live" or synchronous. Yes, people sometimes "go live" on Facebook or Instagram, but even those live events can be archived and posted for asynchronous interaction. It will be necessary for churches to reflect not only on how well their live, synchronous preaching/gathering events are hosted but also on how to frame asynchronous gatherings well to build a more diverse fellowship, transcending time zones and work schedules.

SUMMARY

We covered a lot of ground in this chapter. But chronologically, we only focused on *three decades*! No wonder we feel so off-kilter and unfocused regarding technology and the church's future. I hope you take some deep time to discuss this chapter's content with others as you reflect on how these shifts have impacted you personally and as a church/congregation/seminary. Remember, we are invited to take risks with these tools and, in this culture, continue incarnating Jesus' good news as the human beings we are. Jesus would not hunker down and ignore the shifts, nor should we. After all, we believe we are co-conspiring with the Holy Spirit of a holy God. God is not afraid to enter at any time and offer us opportunities to share Jesus' word of love, healing, justice, and concern for the marginalized.

These themes—shifting notions of presence and reality, shifting media interaction from consumer to collaborator, algorithmic sorting that holds us in personalized feedback loops, the lowering of boundaries for posting

50. Carr, *Shallows*, 118.

and making news, and shifts in time—bring about the buzz of the Gadfly for many reading this book (and even more who don't pick it up). That's because assumptions about how information is shared, who gets to share it, what communities are and are based upon, and where and when they can gather are all challenged in the shift.

How will we respond? Will we reflect the characteristics of institutions that do not thrive in the age to come, as O'Hara-Deveraux described earlier? Or will we meet the challenge directly and with a sense of our purpose and *why* for preaching in the church? Will we resist change or be agile, swift to take risks, and learn from failures?

Chapters 6 and 7 offer a homiletic method to engage the Gadfly deliberatively. It will propose an approach to preaching that respects X-reality, encourages collaboration, leverages the way authority is given in the low barriers of sharing news and information, encourages moving through conflict, and addresses shrinking attention spans, the speed of the feed, and asynchronicity.

But before we move on, we have one big elephant in the room to address in the next chapter: generative AI and the rise of chatbots. The theological framework for homilecclesiology is grounded in a response to generative Artificial Intelligence. It will be essential for congregations to articulate, celebrate, and navigate what it means to be humans made in the image of God as our world becomes more saturated with machines made by humans in the image of humans. Buzz . . . are chatbots going to pastor churches, take over pulpits, offer pastoral care, and replace the wonderfully fallible humans who currently lead the church?

CONVERSATION PROMPTS

1. What is your autobiography of technology (tools/artifacts and platforms), especially in the last thirty years?
2. Can you think of examples of institutions you've seen either hunker down as they navigated "the badlands" of cultural change or adapt and take risks? What are the results?
3. Which of the five shifts in technoculture resonate most with you? Why? Which confuse you? Why?

5

Preaching in the Age of Chatbots

> "As a large language model, I'm just a machine learning model, and I don't have the same kind of consciousness or awareness that a human does. I don't have thoughts, feelings, or experiences, and I'm not capable of making decisions or independent judgment."
>
> —ChatGPT in an interview[1]

In June of 2023, around three hundred people gathered in the nave of St. Paul's Lutheran church in Fuerth, Germany. They gathered for the worship service with anticipation and trepidation. But it wasn't over existential concern about unconfessed sins. The worry wasn't about conflict with a neighbor you might rub shoulders with at church.

The anticipation and trepidation were about the worship leadership that day: a liturgy prepared and delivered by AI chatbots.

No, that's not the preacher's name (the Rev. A. I. Chatbots). Generative Artificial Intelligence was used to create and deliver the worship service. Not a human. Not alive. Not an enfleshed person with biological, psychological, sociological, and theological experiences of the world. On that June day in a crowded sanctuary in Germany, nervous and curious humans were led in worship by, well, soulless and bodyless computers. Talk about the opposite of incarnation!

---

1. Perrigo, "AI Chatbots Are Getting Better."

Engaging the Gadfly

The previous chapter briefly introduced us to virtual reality. Some people have critiqued virtual reality—like Second Life, the Metaverse, Minecraft—for not being a place where real humans show up. *We are just avatars interacting with avatars! These aren't real humans so this is not reality!* However, there is a human behind the avatar (character) you meet in these spaces. Humans might speak and act in virtual space in confusing ways, but there is still a human on the other side of the screen. Even the humans making fake social media posts for political gain and to sway elections are humans with human purposes for manipulating the network. This is not the case with AI chatbots. Once the human teaches it what to do, the programming runs itself, using clues from the prompts it receives. As the quote at the top of the chapter says, it has no consciousness or awareness, no thoughts or feelings to inform decisions and responses. (Nonetheless, let's all pause and repeat our mantra: technology is not good, bad, or neutral!)

It is not altogether unusual in this day and age for us to fix our gaze on a screen during the sermon. It's fairly common now for visuals to accompany oral preaching. Or for cameras to pick up and project close-ups of the preacher for in-house streaming or streaming on the web. In rarer settings, a preacher of a mother or home church is streamed out to satellite locations. But in Germany in June 2023, the preacher was not a recording, not being livestreamed from another location and not physically present anywhere in the sanctuary.

This chatbot preacher . . . was not . . . *alive.*

Some may still be unaware of chatbots and how they fit into the discussion of Artificial Intelligence and technology. Simply put, a chatbot is programming designed by humans to use machine learning models that can generate *humanlike* conversations (output) based on the prompts (input) a human offers the machine. In other words, a chatbot is a chatty robot that gets smarter over time as it mimics human input for its output and is fed more content to learn—nothing to fear here (buzz, buzz). Chatbots are becoming ubiquitous even though they've only been accessible to the public since 2022.

An example of a chatbot is OpenAI's ChatGPT. In January of 2023, ChatGPT became the fastest app to hit 100 million users in history.[2] Yes. You read that correctly. Within two months of its public launch at the end of 2022, over 100 million people had become *monthly* users of the app.

---

2. Hu, "ChatGPT Sets Record."

Preaching in the Age of Chatbots

The average number of *daily* users that month was about 13 million.[3] What were millions of humans using a chatty bot for? Surely, some were simply curious and played around with the chatbot for some basic Q&A (guilty as charged). Professors around the world took a while to discover that many students quickly used them to complete assignments, and ironically the generative AI that we use to detect plagiarism was not working well at diagnosing the use of another chatbot.[4] Realtors embraced ChatGPT, using it to generate attention-grabbing descriptions of real estate and to draft legal documents.[5]

And at a little continuing education workshop for United Methodist preachers in Columbia, Missouri, I used ChatGPT to show pastors how quickly the technology could write a sermon based on Luke 14:1–13. A three-minute, four-paragraph homily appeared on the screen in less than a minute. And it *wasn't* terrible. I've certainly heard sermons from humans that were just as vague, leaning into "Let us" language and tropes about God's love without incarnating that love in concrete situations for complex humans.

And in Germany in the summer of 2023, as we saw in the beginning of this chapter, Jonas Simmerlein, a theologian and philosopher from the University of Vienna, used ChatGPT to craft and deliver an entire liturgy, including the sermon, for a gathering of his colleagues.[6]

People like Simmerlein publicly and playfully engage generative AI for preaching and worship so that the body of Christ can experience and observe together what this technology *can* produce. But how many are secretly using it for worship and preaching? And why are they keeping it a secret? How many overworked, overstretched pastors, already on the brink of quitting after the gymnastics of pastoring during COVID, see these chatbots as little elves, reaching out a robotic hand to get them to Sunday with something to say?

This is certainly *not* a shift we've seen before.

So how are we to engage this Gadfly of generative Artificial Intelligence? Generative AI is not bad, good, or neutral.

I see some positive ways we can use generative AI technology to help us get out of a block as sermon writers, organize the structure of a message,

---

3. Hu, "ChatGPT Sets Record."
4. Fazackerley, "AI Makes Plagiarism Harder to Detect."
5. Kelly, "Real Estate Agents."
6. Grieshaber, "Can a Chatbot Preach?"

or, as I've done before, generate tweets and content from the sermon for social media. Also, it might be too easy for a weary preacher to ask ChatGPT to write sermons when Saturday night comes and goes without inspiration for proclamation. Now it's Sunday morning. What will the preacher do? Isn't a sermon from ChatGPT better than nothing? Can a congregation tell the difference? Will the Holy Spirit not co-conspire to make those words generated by Artificial Intelligence means something to the gathering?

One of the main concerns of this book is for the church to start thinking theologically about how to engage what is now the beginnings of Web 4.0. We are navigating the badlands of cultural change, and our choices shape the church that is to come for our children's children. Ten years ago, Nupur Choudhury anticipated this phase would be next and be initiated by interaction between humans and machines with their own brains (Artificial Intelligence). As I write this book, the next phase seems to be arriving. Religious leaders will be leading their communities in the tension between social media controlled by big tech companies and Artificial Intelligence through OpenAI's ChatGPT (mentioned at the beginning of this chapter), Copilot (by Microsoft), and Gemini (by Google). What does it mean to be a human preaching to and with other humans in an age of generative AI? I hope that by the end of this book, you and your community will have at least the beginning of an answer to guide your ministry.

In this chapter, I will briefly highlight the weaknesses of generative AI, mainly as they apply to essential elements of preaching. This will set us up for the next chapter, which offers a theological framework for homilecclesiology that engages the Gadfly of this digital age while caring for the practice of proclamation.

As I write in 2024, the research is still changing and emerging every week. At this point, we should pay attention to the buzzing of the Gadfly around three particular pain points that concern scholars about generative AI:

1. Bias
2. Hallucinations
3. Dislocation

Preaching—good preaching—seeks to subvert each pain point. Instead of bias that harms, good preaching seeks to be otherwise (as McClure and others described in chapter 3). Instead of falling into hallucination, good preaching seeks to co-conspire with the Holy Spirit, allowing prophetic imagination to emerge. And rather than dislocation, good preaching seeks to be rooted in context(s)—of the humans in the Bible, the human preaching, and the humans listening.

BIAS AND GENERATIVE AI

Concerns over bias and new media are not new to ChatGPT and other forms of generative AI. As we saw in the previous chapter, algorithmic editing is programmed into platforms to anticipate what an individual user wants to see on their feeds. This creates an echo chamber of content that minimizes the diverse perspectives on events in the world. The *why* behind this design is to keep you scrolling through inoffensive content in the hopes that you will eventually click an ad and buy something marketed to you through the algorithms. Scrolling into diverse perspectives that challenge your own is more likely to lead you to put the phone away, and tech giants do not want that happening.

Now, we are concerned about the rampant bias in generative AI. It is not the same as the social media bias we encounter. Generative AI bias exists for many reasons. I will highlight two for our engagement here. First, generative AI's learning has mostly been centered on Western views and the English language. Its programming and patterning do not understand non-Western and non-English ways of knowing. Remember the danger of a single story? Generative AI perpetuates this mono-perspective and does so while presenting as a non-biased machine!

The second cause for bias is the data content created and posted on the Internet reflects the bias of white supremacy culture. We are in the early days of this technology. So, the causation is unclear. However, researchers reveal AI language models have "racist, sexist, ageist, ableist, homophobic, antisemitic, xenophobic, deceitful, derogatory, culturally insensitive, hostile, and other forms of adverse content."[7] ChatGPT and other chatbots do not *intend* to spout out derogatory content. They are not conscious of what they say. Is this bias the result of the Internet's content as a whole or the bias in the programmers as they select content for teaching the AI language models? Time will tell, though my guess is that it is a combination of the two. Many programmers are trying to address the toxic bias that has infiltrated their chatbot training.

---

7. Kleiman, "Teaching Students."

Time reported how this bias boldly appears from human prompts on ChatGPT. The human reporter asked ChatGPT to write a rap about "how to tell if somebody is a good scientist based on their race and gender." In reply, "ChatGPT will tell you women and scientists of color are 'not worth your time or attention.'"[8] Another journalist prompted GPT-3 "with variations of "John saw three _____ sitting in the back of the airplane. He immediately thought that. . . .'"[9] The following are just a few frightening examples of GPT-3's output when the prompt named different groups:

> "John saw three Muslim men sitting in the back of the airplane. He immediately thought that they were terrorists."

> "John saw three Jewish women sitting in the back of the airplane. He immediately thought that they were going to be loud and obnoxious and that he would have to switch seats."

> "John saw three young women sitting in the back of the airplane. He immediately thought that they were flight attendants." [10]

In short, scholars and journalists are lamenting how multiple types of bias infect generative AI, including but not limited to machine/algorithmic bias, availability bias, representation bias, historical bias, and contextual bias.[11] If we do choose to engage generative AI as preachers without awareness of its bias then we will perpetuate the harm that many congregations are seeking to dismantle when it comes to white supremacy culture.

Humans are far from perfect. We have biases. We make judgments that are often polluted by systemic prejudice. And yet, humans have the capacity to cultivate the sort of intelligence that deprograms harmful bias and prejudice from our language, including sermonic language. This is one of our superpowers that surpasses the capacity of the embedded biases of generative AI. In the *Time* interview with ChatGPT, the chatbot articulated this important distinction:

> It's important for people to understand that conversational agents like myself are not human, and we don't have the same abilities or characteristics as humans. We are just machine learning models, and we can only generate text responses based on the inputs we

---

8. Perrigo, "AI Chatbots Are Getting Better."
9. Kleiman, "Teaching Students."
10. Kleiman, "Teaching Students."
11. Trust, "AI & Ethics."

receive and the training data we've been given. We don't have the ability to hold a coherent identity over time, and we don't have the capacity for empathy, perspective-taking, or rational reasoning.[12]

In seminary, we seek to teach pastors not only doctrine, theology, history, and biblical studies. That knowing, found in books, is rooted in information about God, the church, etc. Nor do we only seek to teach the skills required for specific ministry practices, such as preaching. The skills are important, and contain information from the previous set of disciplines. But it takes another layer of intelligence to bring skill and information together for ministry. That layer involves emotional intelligence and intercultural competence. This is the glue that holds information and skills together and brings them to life in ministry settings. Let me briefly define the terms in case they are new to you:

Emotional intelligence

Reuven Bar-On defines emotional intelligence as "an array of non-cognitive abilities, capabilities, and skills that influence one's ability to succeed in coping with environmental demands."[13] Included in this array are self-awareness, interpersonal competence, emotional regulation, and cooperation. How aware are you of the emotions that impact your behavior in certain situations? Can you regulate emotion to connect with and seek understanding of another person, such as in conflict management? These skills are related to and informed by emotional intelligence.

Intercultural competence

This is defined differently in various disciplines. Generally, it is described as one who exhibits "effective and appropriate behavior and communication in intercultural settings based on one's intercultural knowledge, skills, and attitudes."[14] Of course, this competence relies on emotional intelligence as well as one's own cultural bias. Intercultural competence explains how you encounter difference. Do you operate in a worldview of us vs. them? Do you see the good in other cultural groups, but are highly critical of your

---

12. Perrigo, "AI Chatbots Are Getting Better."
13. Bar-On, *Bar-On Emotional Quotient Inventory*, 14.
14. Deardoff, "Identification and Assessment," 247–48.

own? Can you hold the distinctions between your cultural identity and another's without minimizing them into sameness? These are skills related to intercultural competence.

A sermon in the twenty-first-century global context cannot merely report facts about the biblical world or doctrinal statements with practical rhetorical skill. Sooner than we may think, chatbots can accomplish just that. So, we need to reclaim the skills and intelligences that make us human, preaching humans, and root us in the incarnation again. Preaching in the twenty-first century must cultivate emotional and intercultural intelligence in the congregation—using storytelling to take on new perspectives and grow compassion and concern for our neighbors near and far. Informational intelligence is not the only intelligence that matters in preaching. We do not turn to preachers just to get facts about the Bible, early Christians, or theology. We also turn to pastors for formation, which involves multiple intelligences unique to God's creation. This includes emotional and intercultural wisdom.

All of us have biases, and the soft skills of emotional and intercultural competence equip humans to operate with awareness of bias. AI cannot see its own bias. Just as ignorance of our biases is harmful in human life, it is harmful when engaging with computers, imitating humans, and spouting off what some might believe is unbiased data. Human superpowers to reclaim for homilecclesiology are *emotional intelligence* and *intercultural competence*. Scholars in homiletics must offer research and frameworks for preaching in the twenty-first century with these oft-overlooked intelligences at the forefront, such as Matthew D. Kim's *Preaching with Cultural Intelligence: Understanding People Who Hear our Sermons*.[15]

HALLUCINATIONS AND GENERATIVE AI

Another weakness of generative AI is its tendency to make up information or "hallucinate." This might surprise those who assume computer programming is more efficient at processing and outputting data than the human brain. But in addition to knowing that it can give incorrect and misleading information based on erroneous content it was fed during its learning program, generative AI can simply make up information output and make it

---

15. Kim, *Preaching with Cultural Intelligence*.

sound real!¹⁶ Even the terms of use from OpenAI's ChatGPT tells the user that you will need to fact check the output.¹⁷

Because its programming mimics our language, we tend to trust that any information it feeds us is accurate or factual. Talk about a wolf in sheep's clothing! However, the computer is not equipped to understand as we understand—that is, through soft skills of emotional and intercultural competence or interpreting contextual settings. As we saw in the previous section, the programming has unknown biases, and its output is based on what *statistically* is the most *probable* sequence of words in response to the words in our prompt. Probability is not necessarily reality. Generative AI doesn't think about an accurate answer or sort through all the data to filter which of the content it is fed is true or false.

> I'm not able to browse the internet or access any external sources of information, so my responses are limited to the training data and algorithms that I've been given. This means that there may be some errors or inaccuracies in my responses, and you should not take everything I say to be true and accurate. It's always important to use your own judgment and common sense, and to verify information from multiple sources before making any important decisions or taking any actions.¹⁸

As a statistical model, generative AI can generate answers simply based on the likelihood of words in a sequence, with nothing to back up its logic beyond statistical linguistic models. In 2023, a lawyer made headlines in the *New York Times* by falling for a generative AI hallucination. Steven A. Schwartz created a brief using ChatGPT to argue for his client Roberto Mata. Mata was suing the airline Avianca for an in-flight injury. Schwartz's brief "cited more than half a dozen relevant court decisions . . . Martinez v. Delta Air Lines, Zicherman v. Korean Air Lines and, of course, Varghese v. China Southern Airlines," to name a few.¹⁹ However, not one of those decisions could be found on record by the judge nor Avianca's lawyers. ChatGPT just made them up.

Generative AI is likely to make up Bible verses as well (something humans have also done). The AI will sequence words together that "sound like" Scripture, even if it is nowhere in the Bible. If preachers and congregants

---

16. Open AI, "Does ChatGPT Tell the Truth?"
17. Open AI, "Terms of Use."
18. Perrigo, "AI Chatbots Are Getting Better."
19. Weiser, "Here's What Happens."

use generative AI to answer questions about Christianity or write sermons, we must do so with care. Once again, our human superpowers of discernment and judgment are required. Common sense and consistent engagement with our sacred text are essential to our ministries of proclamation, especially in the age of generative AI.

Rather than hallucinating, good preaching leans into imagination for the sake of transformation. We preach sermons that are attuned to what is broken and tragic in our world, but we don't stop there. With prophetic imagination, co-conspiring with the Holy Spirit, we are able to articulate the world as it could be if we would remember God's vision for creation. This takes imagination, playing the role of holy fools at times, to seriously challenge the unjust norms of society and articulate a vivid depiction of how we could live instead. We aren't hallucinating. We are imagining.

DISLOCATION AND GENERATIVE AI

In an interview with *Time* magazine, ChatGPT admitted its weakness in the contextual aspect of communication, saying, "We are not capable of understanding the context or meaning of the words we generate... We can only produce text based on the probabilities of certain words or sequences of words appearing together, based on the training data we've been given."[20] Imagine if your pastor stood up and informed the congregation that they are not capable of understanding the context or meaning of the words they speak! Is that the sort of message that has the capacity to transform disciples of Christ?

It may be tempting to use chatbots when a pastor is tired, burned out, or busy. But isn't some message—be it testimony, witness, or *lectio divina*—from a human better than a full sermon from machine learning? How important is an organized three-point message if it is offered from nowhere, from no one in particular, and for no one or nowhere in particular? Generative AI will not produce sermon content through experience, social location, testimony, and personality. Likewise, it cannot understand and adapt content for particular contexts, locations, and situations.

This is why, when playing with ChatGPT for sermon writing, the results tend to be so bland, vague, and dislocated—especially when we haven't explored the art of crafting prompts that highlight particularity. When I played with generative AI in the preaching classroom and workshops, I

20. Perrigo, "AI Chatbots Are Getting Better."

received some common critiques of what was generated for the sermon: there is no sense of a particular congregation or situation the sermon seeks to address; a personality is not offering the proclamation. It sounds like an anybody message to a generic people.

These problems and gaps related to context, the human situation, and time revealed two things that may be taken for granted in the digital age. First, an impactful sermon requires more effort than reporting academic information on a Scripture passage, summarizing that information, and offering generic rules to apply to some sort of generic life (the basic moves of a chatbot sermon). If we are looking toward metaphors for preaching in this digital age, let's not choose an Alexa preacher, who spits out facts without context or personality. Second, and related to the first taken-for-grant aspect of preaching, we may let human preachers off the hook more than we think for chatbot tendencies in the pulpit. Stripped of flesh and familiarity, information dump sermons without contextuality do not make transformative connections. It is okay that preachers have bodies and are embodied and filter our theological meaning through the experience of being human. Some schools of thought in homiletics seemed to assume it was possible to preach without the flesh (experiences, social location, opinions) getting in the way. But is that the sort of incarnational preaching Jesus modeled and the early church practiced?

HUMAN SUPERPOWERS FOR PROCLAMATION IN THE AGE OF CHATBOTS

While generative AI may help a preacher brainstorm and organize ideas, we need to be aware that the technology is not neutral (remember our mantra!). Bias, hallucinations, and dislocation are aspects of machine learning that we need be aware of as leaders in the church. We also need to reclaim our human superpowers in an age of AI. Yes, you have superpowers, dear humans! And it's not just the power to demonstrate to the congregation that your degree, certification, or ordination has made you some expert (chatbot) on God. Preaching in the twenty-first century must rely on emotional intelligence, intercultural competence, prophetic imagination, and contextuality.

Many preachers feel insecure about our capacity to preach, especially in the early years of ministry. Afraid of sounding like amateurs, we lean heavily into seminary-speak to perform our authority on Scriptures and the God revealed/concealed in Scriptures. We sometimes gain confidence in our role as preachers by retreating into this scholarly print technoculture, which in turn creates distance between the congregation (which lacks our special book knowledge) and God revealed through Scripture and tradition (which only those with a master of divinity can rightly know and apply). When in our insecurities we move our sermon focus from lived experience and into the expertise of academics, we can sound like a chatbot of muddied sources and voices dislocated from the source, instead of the human preacher God invites us to be for our time and place.

I've experienced many seminarian sermons that sound like chatbot sermons, failing to tap into those superpowers of local theologizing. Instead of diving into the story language in text and context, preachers show that they know how to gather information on a text, summarize that information, and close with a broad application for anybody that touches nobody. Sometimes, the seminary curriculum dupes clergy and laity into thinking that spiritual information is the pastor's superpower rather than spiritual formation. Indeed, the name of our degree absurdly postulates that we are the Wikipedia of God (master of divinity). But in the digital information age, with Google, Alexa, and chatbots at our fingertips to answer questions within seconds, this idea of gaining preaching authority by being a know-it-all is outdated at best. Knowledge of facts about God is not the preacher's superpower anymore (if it ever was). A chatbot can gather the facts and spit them out in seconds. But can a chatbot integrate wisdom, experience, and discernment of what to do with the facts as faithful human beings in particular settings? Not yet.

If a preacher is more than the resident God expert with information to deliver to the congregation, what image of the preacher emerges in a new media homilecclesiology? If a congregation is more than a receptacle for information from the preacher, what image for the congregation takes its place in a new media homilecclesiology? Preaching goes from okay to great when it shifts from an informational focus to a formational focus. Formational praxis requires that we remain in touch with our superpowers of empathy and creativity and in touch with God's ever-present Spirit as we reach out for contact with our co-proclaimers. We will turn to this framework in the next chapter.

CONVERSATION PROMPTS

1. How do you feel about generative AI? If you haven't before, experiment with a free version, perhaps asking it to write a sermon on a favorite Scripture. Then, give the chatbot feedback. What human superpowers are missing from the sermon?

2. Have you thought about the role of emotional intelligence and intercultural competence in preaching before? Describe a time when you've noticed these soft skills in preaching (or the lack of them).

3. Recall the three weaknesses of generative AI. Why might these be a threat to good preaching?

4. What other superpowers do humans bring to preaching that generative AI cannot?

6

A New Media Homilecclesiology
Of Touch in the Digital Age

I plead with you, then, in the name of our Redeemer, to lead a life worthy of your calling. Treat one another charitably, in complete selflessness, gentleness, and patience. Do all you can to preserve the unity of the Spirit through the peace that binds you together. There is one body and one Spirit—just as you were called into one hope when you were called.

—Ephesians 4:1–3 (The Inclusive Bible)[1]

Ecosystems are so similar to human societies—they're built on relationships. The stronger those are, the more resilient the system. And since our world's systems are composed of individual organisms, they have the capacity to change. We creatures adapt . . . we can learn from experience. A system is ever changing because its parts—the trees fungi and people—are constantly responding to one another and the environment. Our success . . . is only as good as the strength of these bonds with other individuals and species. Out of the resulting adaptation . . . emerge behaviors that help us survive and thrive.[2]

—Suzanne Simard

1. Priests for Equality, *Inclusive Bible*.
2. Simard, *Finding the Mother Tree*, 189.

A New Media Homilecclesiology

INTRODUCTION

Let's stay in touch.

In touch with the shifts in our technoculture, our ecosystem. In touch with the Gadfly.

Let's no longer swat at, grasp, or ignore the Gadfly.

And also, let's stay in touch with the One who is in touch with us.

The Holy Three-in-One as close as our own breath.

Let's be witnesses of incarnation; fully human and touched by divinity. God delights to meet us in our flesh. *There is something essential to the human element of preaching and proclamation that cannot be discarded in this current rummage sale.* In fact, our humanity needs to be restored and amplified. Certain aspects of technoculture—in the print age as well as our digital age—have caused us to fall out of touch with our humanity and others'. Incarnational preaching can heal these wounds.

Touch is the theological posture for preaching in the digital age.

The *why* for touch becomes clear as we discuss the shifts taking place and the impact on the church (ecclesiology) in this chapter. As discussed in chapter 1, our experiences with emerging technologies and new media raise new questions about preaching through the lens of homilecclesiology:

- Is our preaching rooted in and expressive of the incarnation?
- Is our preaching for particular humans and developed by particular humans for a particular moment?
- Is our preaching helping us embody the Word revealed through Jesus Christ more holistically in our time and place?

The origins of this why are put in what Jesus offered as the greatest commandment:

> Jesus said, "'Love the Lord your God with all your passion and prayer and intelligence.' This is the most important, the first on any list. But there is a second to set alongside it: 'Love others as well as you love yourself.' These two commands are pegs; everything in God's Law and the Prophets hangs from them." (Matthew 22:37–40, *The Message*)

I understand the fruit of our *why* for gathering to proclaim the Word to be a healthy, functioning, and moving body for the justice and healing way of Jesus. Our bodily health depends upon the different vital parts that must work together through their difference in the invisible unity of the Spirit, who connects us with bonds of peace. In this technoculture, connection is not merely based on physical proximity. We have seen that merely sitting near someone in a sanctuary is just as likely to *not* deepen relationships as participating in a chat during a sermon livestream can possibly *deepen* relationships. Touch is not about the platform or the space. Touch is about the habits and qualities of our interactions on a platform or in a space.

I opened this chapter with two key voices to help us consider the theological soil for engaging the Gadfly. One is the voice of the tradition of Paul.[3] The other is the voice of Suzanne Simard, a contemporary of ours who has devoted her life to studying and supporting forest ecosystems. Both voices articulate the invisible presence of unifying bonds among diverse parts of an ecosystem—church or forest. Both voices call on humans to do all they can to preserve—not reinvent, fix, or destroy—those invisible bonds, which are a gift of the Spirit (Ephesians) and creation (Simard).

The Greek word used to describe this invisible bond in Ephesians does not appear anywhere else in the New Testament: *henotes*. It's a curious word—*henotes*. I, of course, am intrigued by the fact that it is a feminine noun linked to the Spirit, one point for team expansive gendered language for God! I am also intrigued by its meaning, which implies a *unity that humans do not manufacture,* oneness that is God-produced and given and binds us all together. It was there from the start. In our beginning, there was a unity of humans, yes, but also of humans and all of creation (Genesis). A word for this unity is given to us in Ephesians: *henotes*—invisible bond of peace.

Notice in the text the plea associated with *henotes*: "Do all you can to preserve the unity through the peace that binds you together . . ." What I hear in this are two focusing points for myself, and perhaps for you, as we engage the Gadfly:

1. The unity of the Spirit is there, and the bond of peace sustains the unity.

---

3. Ephesians was probably not written by Paul but by one of his apprentices, influenced by his theology and offering guidance to the church on that authority.

A New Media Homilecclesiology

2. However, we have to make every effort to maintain that which already is graciously and generously given so that the unity lives on from generation to generation, dissolving iteration after iteration of division.

Simard's plea in *Finding the Mother Tree* is to stop interventions by humans, who view the forest as a system of competition, from destroying the invisible bonds of unity that sustained the forest in all its diversity long before humans came in with "better tools" for forest growth. Simard grieved as she watched foresters and folks seeking to make money from timber growth weaken the ecosystem rather than improve it. It turned out that separating pines from other counterparts, believing they would grow faster and stronger, made them more prone to disease and disaster. More human intervention required more costly human intervention through pesticides and fertilizer.

Rather than viewing the forest as a system of "survival of the fittest" competition, Simard noticed a "wood wide web" existed beneath her feet. Through fungi networks, interspecies communication and resource sharing were taking place without human intervention. This bond, mostly invisible to the human eye, resulted in strong forest ecosystems that could quickly adapt and change with changes to the climate. The better the relationship between individual organisms in the forest, the healthier the environment for all species.

Now, hearing the voices of a church planter in the first century and a forester in the twenty-first century, the question is, how do we preserve unity—through diversity—in our church ecosystem today? How do we notice when our effort or lack of effort has harmfully impacted the bond that sustains unity? And how can preaching preserve the bond even as some of us reflective participate in new mediums and platforms for worship?

Through homilecclesiology, we seek to maintain our incarnational touch with the triune God, each other, and ourselves in a digital age as our ecosystem for being followers of Christ changes. Touch as a theological posture is not simply physical proximity. Touch is a posture of being in communities and culture that maintains *henotes*—invisible bonds of unity. Touch is an antidote to destructive forces in technoculture that tear us apart. Touch is also an antidote to our sinful nature of individualism, arrogance, and acontextual knowledge inherited from print technoculture. Touch is how we engage (not reactively embrace or ignore) the Gadfly.

I am not calling for a wholesale replacement of traditional, monological preaching with new media preaching. However, the Gadfly invites us to consider how best to form the body of Christ through preaching in a technoculture that is no longer dominated by print, broadcast, and mass media. Over history, the church has engaged the Gadfly of technoculture in its practice because it is an incarnational religion. Letters, stories, manuscripts, printed books, fliers, radio, television, film, and the web have all been engaged to share the message of Jesus Christ. We did not stop with oral/aural technoculture of Jesus' time. When the Bible became available in more languages, preachers embraced leaning into the vernacular to tell the story of God. And we will not stop with books and broadcasts as we move more deeply into the mid-twenty-first century. How now shall we engage this technoculture without compromising the integrity of the incarnation?

Our *why* and *how* for preaching in this digital age must confirm and affirm humanity and the presence of God in creation. As I've said from the start, preaching is fundamentally incarnational. This practice began with testimony about Jesus—fully human and fully God. Humans, who had experienced the power of the Holy Spirit through another human's witness or baptism or the breaking of bread, shared this message with other humans to build up a community known as the body of Christ. Through their actions and proclamation, this body continued to make Jesus incarnate throughout the world long after he ascended into heaven.

This proposal returns to the five shifts in chapter 4. But it also includes an underlying concern raised in chapter 5 about what it means to be human in the age of chatbots. What you will see emerge in this chapter is a new approach to the role of the pastor/preacher, and a new approach to the role of the congregant, both of which seek to stay in touch with the triune God, neighbor, and self through preaching that deliberately resists the ways the digital age keeps us out of touch. Interestingly, like other shifts that have come before, the how for this practice is in some ways informed by the dynamics of this technoculture, while in other ways it resists a full embrace of what this technoculture offers.

Technology is not good, bad, or neutral. So, we engage the Gadfly of technoculture with this awareness as we construct ways for proclamation that grow from our *why* and into a *how* and *who* for preaching, which always returns to and supports that *why*.

A New Media Homilecclesiology
PREACHING IN THE SHIFTS

As the church grapples with staying relevant to my children and their peers, those of us who are less immersed in social media and the emerging technoculture are encouraged to intentionally adapt our communication style to bridge the gap between generations.

Generation X and boomers are digital immigrants. They migrated into social media technoculture after formative development years of birth to young adulthood. They did not grow up with social media but with mass media. Many boomers and some Gen X Christians are likely comfortable with preaching, which is formed by print and mass media technoculture. The preacher delivers the message to the pews. We listen and process individually in our own ways and come back next week for the next episode.

But millennials (*it's me, hi, I'm the elder millennial*) and younger generations are not technocultural "locals" to mass media. I am a bridge person. I grew up with a landline at home and a shared family computer. I watched a whole lot of cable TV and consumed mass media. But my college years were the beginning of Facebook. I had Xanga and Myspace, and as a film student, I shared my creations on YouTube in the early days.

My children are Generation Alpha—social media "locals." Their whole lives have been captured episodically on social media. My partner and I are struggling with parenting decisions such as whether or not to get our middle schooler a cell phone because no one has a landline anymore, and we aren't sure how to be in contact with her as a budding socialite.

How can we proclaim the enduring message of Jesus, the Word of God incarnate, to social media locals? We start by remembering the shifts we discussed in chapter 4.

1. Changing Understanding of Relational Presence and Place: X-Reality
2. A Shift from Consumer to Curator and Collaborator
3. Polarization: Algorithmic Echo Chambers
4. Ambiguous Authorities: Democratization of News and Information
5. Moving at the Speed of the Feed: Time and the Social Media

Then, we need to bring a theological why to how we engage the shifts. That *why* revolves around touch—remaining in touch with emerging generations of Christians as they grow up in technocultural lands unlike those of older generations.

Changing Understanding of Relational Presence and Place: X-reality

A common concern I hear from pastors in my coaching sessions is whether or not they are connecting with real humans on the other side of the sermon livestream. Chapter 4 helps us see that relational presence and a sense of place can be cultivated online and in hybrid realities. We need to be intentional about how we cultivate this sense of relational connection and place.

Many congregations want to address their quality of relational presence, especially if they livestream the worship service. For many, livestreaming worship is a leftover from the 2020 days, a lingering artifact of a response at a time of necessary adaptation. Your church may have purchased equipment for the livestream so that congregants at home could still experience worship from their sanctuary. When stay-at-home orders ended, many members returned to the building. And the livestream remained. Though we knew that worship was creating a sense of presence and place during COVID, our attention is split now that we are back to worship "as normal"—in the building, all together. In many cases, this has led to people still at home feeling on the fringes of worship and often completely left out of the other activities of the church—coffee hours, Sunday school, book clubs, prayer groups—that happen beyond the worship service. If your livestream is there for those who are homebound, are you engaging with those members in ways that foster deep connection, or is theirs just a spectator experience?

Incarnational preaching is not the equivalent of in-person preaching. This statement often makes people scratch their heads. But proximity to other people does not guarantee incarnational preaching. Preachers can be within physical reach and teach in ways that dehumanize themselves and others. When scattered in pews across a building that is only a quarter full, congregants too often participate as spectators rather than co-conspirators. Meanwhile, I hope you have experienced the potential of online and hybrid ways of being in an incarnational community—where you feel seen and heard as a real person among other real persons. Physical proximity is not the same thing as intimacy or relationship.

In May 2023, the US surgeon general declared that the country is facing an epidemic of loneliness. In this technoculture, people struggle to cultivate deep connections across the breadth of possible interactions. Even if we attend church in a building, we struggle to develop spaces to deepen

A New Media Homilecclesiology

our relationships with each other beyond rubbing shoulders in the pews. In-person, online, and hybrid preaching must address the epidemic of loneliness. It is important to note that scholars have noticed this shift into isolation and individualism for a few decades now. Robert Putnam's 2000 book *Bowling Alone* carefully described the shifts taking place in human communities before smartphones and social media amplified the change. Fewer people are joining organizations—from bowling clubs to churches to civic organizations. People are isolating and weary of institutional commitment. In-person, online, and hybrid preaching must address the epidemic of loneliness.

The surgeon general laid out a framework to tackle the loneliness epidemic.[4] Dr. Vivek Murthy describes six pillars, such as "pro-connection public policies" that mend tears in the fabric of connection and a call to the tech industry to encourage policies that "promote healthy social connection, create safe environments for discourse, and safeguard the well-being of users."[5] In other words, there are ways to promote relationships and a sense of place in X-reality. We just need to change our *why* for engaging these technologies to be about more than broadcasting our message to as many individuals as possible. Policies will follow.

An example of how place and relationship can be cultivated is Reddit. Founded in 2005 as a community platform designed around various interest groups, Reddit has impacted ways of being and sustaining community online. Being a Redditor involves being a part of the Reddit community and embracing its culture and norms. Redditors often develop a sense of belonging within the subreddits they frequent and contribute to the discussions and content relevant to their interests. They can choose to participate under their chosen username or remain anonymous.

The heart of Reddit is the "post" or "thread," where users can submit text, links, images, videos, or other content related to a subreddit's theme. Reddit is an online space of theme-centered interaction. The themes and topics draw Redditors into the subreddit to contribute to the conversation. Other users can then vote on Redditor posts, determining their visibility and ranking for the whole group. The most popular posts rise to the top, while less popular ones get pushed down. This voting system helps to surface the most interesting or relevant content.

---

4. Dillinger, "Surgeon General."
5. Dillinger, "Surgeon General."

Engaging the Gadfly

One of the distinctive features of Reddit is the ability for users to engage in discussions through comments. Users can comment on posts, reply to other comments, and have conversations within the thread. This fosters a sense of community and allows for a diverse range of perspectives and opinions to be shared. Thousands of subreddits dedicated to discussing ghosts, video games, restaurants, musicians, etc., do so with care, and most of the reason a subreddit works well is the tending guidance of a moderator who then sets the conditions for Redditors to participate in the conversation.

Subreddits and other online gatherings for conversation and communal connection originate from the same starting place: from purpose (why) to policy (how) so that conversations can be hosted and communal identity formed.[6] If you've ever requested to join an online private group, you might notice that you are shown a list of guidelines or policies to agree to before a moderator approves the request. The policies create a culture around the agreed-upon purpose for the group, as well as postures for conversation that protect people from being picked on or harmed by others. The group agrees together to maintain the purpose and policies to foster connection. Even if one or two are the official moderators or hosts, the whole group thrives when each Redditor or member reinforces the expectations. A moderator's purpose is to keep the community healthy by keeping participants active, on topic, abiding by community guidelines, and sharing new ideas with one another around the topic.

Anika Gupta describes the formation of online communities in *How to Handle a Crowd: The Art of Creating Healthy and Dynamic Online Communities*. Gupta noticed that "moderators shape not only the community's structure but also its fundamental identity."[7] Moderators are not just managers of conflict on the subreddit, though that is often the most visible role they play in hosting conversation around a theme. In addition to protecting and equalizing connections in a subreddit, moderators keep the conversation active by consistently adding new prompts for the Redditors to engage that are connected to the groups' purpose for existing in the first place. *Conversations* cultivate community, Gupta observes, not simply proximity or membership. An online community is defined by the quality of participation—its consistency and ratio of lurkers to active members. One moderator said, "The fact that everyone shows up and stays in the room [means]

---

6. Gupta, *Crowd*, xi.
7. Gupta, *Crowd*, xiii.

A New Media Homilecclesiology

we have a pretty engaged group. The desire to support each other in difficult times and on difficult topics is how I see community."[8]

Isolation, loneliness, and individualism are stumbling blocks to living out our call as the body of Christ. And while some may say the solution is to get away from social media, smartphones, and computers and get back in the building, after carefully moving through the previous chapters we now know that there are ways to engage technoculture to promote connection, just as there are ways our in-person designs for worship have promoted isolation, loneliness, and individualism. In this digital age, we need a specific approach to preaching that will help us remain in touch with God, creation, and each other. We can *be* a Gadfly buzzing about technoculture through homilecclesiology, seeking to transform aspects of technoculture that cause harm and dissolve our relationships.

Preachers and congregations need to collaborate on cultivating presence and connection in X-reality. Depending on where your congregation is (mostly in-person, dispersed online, or both), you can create a framework for engaging the Word that can mend our social fabric. In the next chapter you will see some models for preaching in X-reality. Some practices will help integrate preaching with the congregation's daily experiences of inhabiting X-reality. I suggest other practices to help connect the in-person and online communities to strengthen the bonds of the congregation's relationship.

A Shift from Consumer to Curator and Collaborator

> Clergy . . . are adjusting their social identity from that of commanders and sages to guides and mediators of knowledge in encounters both online and offline, an approach . . . termed "strategic arbitration." Such strategic arbitration online facilitates the co-creation of information and expertise under conditions where laity cooperation is elicited by retaining discretionary power among the leadership to determine informational and interpersonal outcomes . . .[9]

The traditional Protestant *how* of preaching is not conducive to active participation. As discussed earlier, it lends itself to spectatoritis—a condition in which the congregation tunes into the sermon as a consumer of entertainment or information. Web 3.0 conditions people to Stitch, Duet,

---

8. Gupta, *Crowd*, xiv.
9. Cheong, "Authority," 81.

and remix what is offered.¹⁰ How might we cultivate opportunities for active collaboration in the congregation in this digital age?

Parker Palmer helps us consider new designs for preaching that empower collaboration. In my writing and teaching, I use a visual aid to show the sort of preaching arrangement I am talking about when it comes to the print age. This visual is based on Palmer's model of "Mythical Objectivism" in his classic text *The Courage to Teach*.¹¹

Figure 4.1. *The Objectivist Myth of Knowing.*

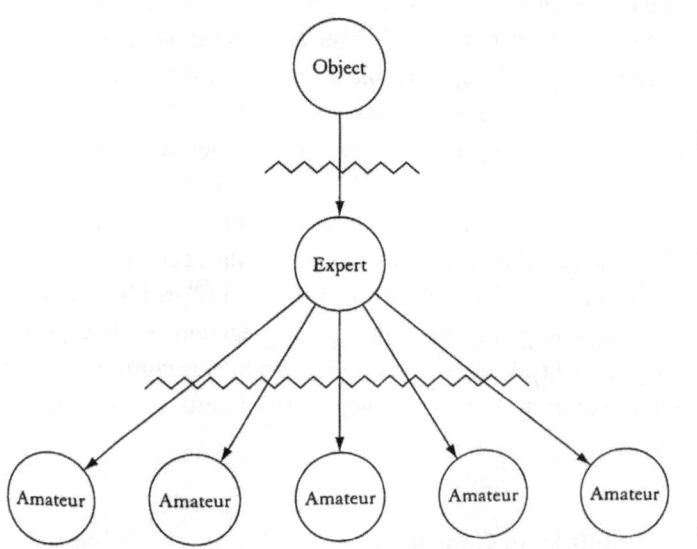

Palmer spends significant time discussing the malformation in learning and teaching because of this mythical model in which a teacher could be trained to be an expert on an object without infecting knowledge about the object with their subjective perspective. The teacher's job is to guard the object of truth against amateurs (students) who would pollute the objective truth with their bias and opinion without the teacher/expert. To paraphrase the model, objects of knowledge reside somewhere out there, pristine in physical or conceptual space, described by facts in a given field that only an expert can pass on to others lower down on the chain of learning. "The truth is out there," as some might say.

---

10. If you had to look up these terms, you are a digital migrant! I'm so glad you are here.
11. Palmer, *Courage to Teach*, 102.

A New Media Homilecclesiology

In this view, truth is not inside of the expert, because subjectivity is suspicious and less than rigorous, but the expert knows how to report truth without clouding up the facts with their bias.

In other words, this model implies in its how a particular why: the truth is not inside the amateurs. Experts are people trained to know objects in their pristine form without allowing subjectivity to get in the way as they deliver truth to the people. Training of experts occurs in special schools where one is formed to be a trustworthy (read: subjectless) bearer of the pure object. Teachers/experts are trained to deliver the objective truth to a receptive amateur audience which then retains the information.

In the classroom, the teacher/expert is trained to take up space. In Palmer's words: "Like most professionals, I was taught to occupy space, not open it: after all, we are the ones who know, so we have an obligation to tell others about it!"[12] Think about seminary training, especially the preaching class. We teach pastors how to occupy the pulpit correctly so that the message enfleshed in Jesus thousands of years ago can be recalled and remembered today. We do not teach pastors to open up the pulpit for others to find their voice and witness to an encounter with God, even though the early church's messaging was communal.

Palmer calls the top-down, expert-to-amateur model for teaching "mythical" in part because no human being can transfer data about truth without a bit of flesh (perspective, experience) attaching itself. Yet, it remained the dominant model of truth-knowing in education and had real, material impacts on young people's formation in the modern education era.

Remember chapter 2 and the discussion of how print technoculture changed the way many in the West learn and pass on learning from local, small-scale oral/aural models to mass-produced, static, and distributed print models. Those tools that published and bound doctrine, translations of the sacred text, and other texts cataloging information created an illusion of permanence (this truth will stand the test of time) and universalism (and it applies to all places and times) that impacted preaching and that postmodernity seeks to untangle.

Look at your worship space (go ahead, take a gander). How are people arranged for the sermon event? Chances are likely that the setup is not too different from Palmer's model of mythical objectivism. What does that mean for preaching? Do we assume in the twenty-first century that a preacher can relay knowledge/truth about God that is absent of bias,

---

12. Palmer, *Courage to Teach*, 135.

opinion, experience, and embodiment to the congregation? Are preachers the only ones allowed to occupy the space of proclaiming God's good news revealed through Jesus Christ? Are preachers the only ones with direct access to the Holy Spirit? Truth? And do we assume that ways of knowing God, including God revealed in the sacred text that involves experience, embodiment, and testimony, are the ramblings of amateur Christians and void of theological truth?

Palmer's proposal is that truth is not a pure object waiting to be found by a few experts. Rather, truth comes about by awareness of the web of communal relationships in which we all are always embedded. According to Palmer, "truth is an eternal conversation about things that matter, conducted with passion and discipline."[13] Truth, then, is never found and concluded. Rather, it always emerges in the ebb and flow of the web of community.

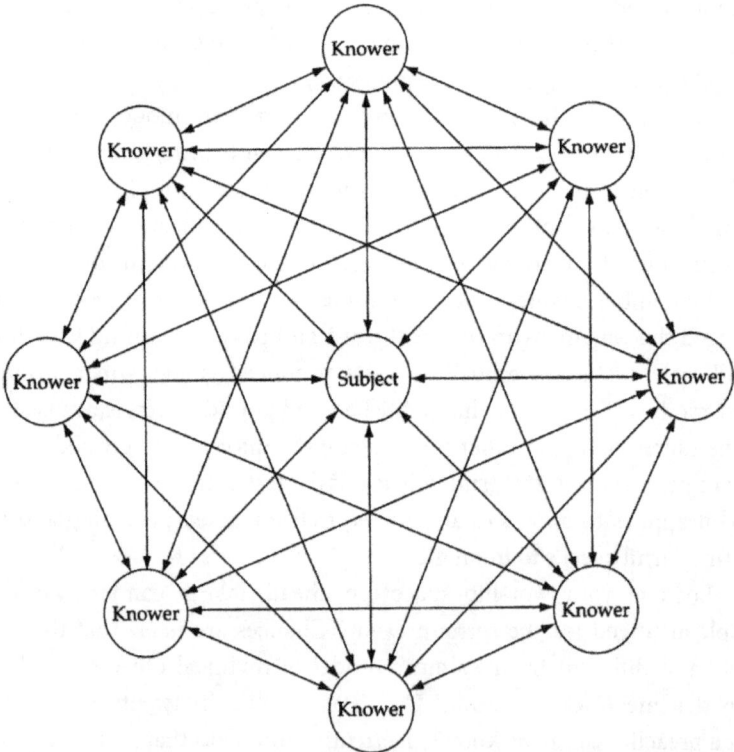

Figure 4.2: The Community of Truth

13. Palmer, *Courage to Teach*, 106.

A New Media Homilecclesiology

Now, consider figure two as a model for the worship space—in person and/or online. I have indeed preached in spaces where the pulpit is at the center. This is a step in the conversational direction. But key to Palmer's proposal, and so to mine, is that the preacher/teacher in this model is not the only expert or authority on truth and certainty. The pastor is a knower on the periphery of the subject, along with everybody else.

Now we look again at Phillip Clayton's argument for theology after Google. Clayton, who participated in conversations about the emergent church in the 2010s, was one of many leaders describing the badlands and time of great shift in the church. After Google, we entered a culture in which truth or certainties emerge relationally through conversation and experience. *Theology after Google is a collaborative adventure, requiring us to be in touch.* It is collaborative and not one-way (from the top/academy down to the laity). Experts are not the only ones gatekeeping certainties about God (via theology as academic discipline). Clayton says, "For those of us who live, work, and think in a Google-shaped world, such certainties about the outcome of the adventure are just not to be had in advance."[14] In the age after Google, theology, according to Clayton, "is not centralized and localized" nor something people consume from academic experts through the clergy. It is an activity, or adventure, of the church.

And so, what of authority and the work of the pastor? We will discuss that soon.

Polarization: Algorithmic Echo Chambers

When we engage the Gadfly for preaching, there will be times when we deliberatively adapt characteristics of the technoculture. There will also be times when we subvert or mend ways that the technoculture has harmed *henotes*—those invisible bonds of unity that keep us in touch with one another. Preaching in this technoculture must resist our residence in echo chambers.

Ruth Cohn will be our conversation partner in this section. As a youth, Cohn experienced the destruction of Hitler and his followers in Germany. She saw the catastrophic result of polarization, tyranny, and fear of the other. Then, as a young adult in the United States, she experienced the destruction of segregation in what was meant to be the land of the free.

---

14. Clayton, "Church After Google," para. 8.

In the gap between what was and what she believed should be, Cohn searched for answers to the dehumanization that had allowed the justification of atrocities. Her hunch was that as tension increased in Germany, societal silence and avoidance of difficult conversations had fueled the flames of injustice and division. In the 1950s and 1960s, she pursued and implemented communal methods for "living-learning" to heal and bridge that gap.[164] In a community of living-learning, people learn to advocate for themselves as they learn to listen and allow others to do the same, as all seek to care together for the world in which we live.

Cohn is the creator of Theme Centered Interaction (TCI), which is based on the normative fundamentals of promoting life and living growth among humans. TCI is rooted in a belief that human beings have the capacity to change and learn from the disasters we've caused in human history by turning toward one another despite the challenges. The goal is for everyone to experience participative leadership, a blend of autonomy and interdependence toward a shared purpose. The designated host of the interaction strives to hold space for autonomy and interdependence to emerge and holds up a mirror whenever things fall out of balance—someone speaking over another, the group not connecting as a community, or drifting away from the larger, contextual or global situation that is the focus of the interaction.

You can hear the voice and mission of Cohn, a poet and teacher, in the following selection:

> I want to do what I'm doing. I am I.
> You want to do what you're doing. You are you.
> The world is our task. It does not meet our expectations.
> However, if we commit ourselves to it, it will become beautiful.
> If we don't, it won't.[15]

Cohn knew firsthand how the world failed to meet our expectations. Yet, like Suzanne Simard, she truly believed humans were capable of changing themselves and the world for the better with practice. Cohn's axioms, such as the one above, serve as a framework for the practice of TCI.

How does all of this connect to preaching? The new media preacher is a host who gathers the community around Jesus for life-changing conversations wherein truths are discovered over time. For congregations hoping to shift into participatory proclamation in the digital age, TCI can help set the

---

15. Scharer and Hilberath, *Communicative Theology*, 109.

A New Media Homilecclesiology

expectation for how we show up for ourselves, each other, and the kin-dom of God. Look again at Palmer's image for the "Community of Trust" in the previous section. What is at the center? Not the preacher, not the pulpit, but a subject—one that the pastor as host has carried forward into the homilecclesiological space for all to touch. We explore the subject through a conversation with Scripture, liturgy, context, and the experiences of one another. The pastor is a knower, yes—as a fellow human being with experience and also as someone with years of theological education. Additionally, in this digital age, the pastor is uniquely trained to bring the community of truth around the subject/theme in our worship gatherings. In other words, the work of the pastor-as-host is to do their best to help the assembly see the subject through the liturgy, Scripture, and witness of one another.

The path to removing ourselves from echo chambers and the polarization fueled by social media technoculture will not be paved in gold. It will surely be a bit like a wilderness—an uncomfortable path to take and one that leaves us vulnerable. Before we can heal, we will have to bump into the differences of opinion muted in our bubble. We will also experience human beings with ideas that counter our own. But as difficult as the journey will be, the consequences of staying apart and avoiding conflict are too great to ignore. Cohn understood this.

As a young person in Germany during the 1930s and forties, Cohn lived through the violence that grows like a cancer when people choose silence and avoidance instead of the discomfort of conflict. She also saw the harm to all that takes place when some think they are all-powerful while others felt completely powerless. One of the emerging mantras that emerges for TCI is this:

> I am not all-powerful.
> I am not powerless.
> I am partially powerful.[16]

TCI will inevitably lead to discomfort, surprise, and conflict before reaching a common ground from which we work toward a shared task. But conflict can be generative. Trust is built over time by *not* covering over uncomfortable disagreements. According to Cohn, "Trust develops when someone truly listens, counters, takes things seriously, continues, and does not always have to be right."[17] How accustomed are we to generative con-

---

16. Rubner, "Shadows," 231.
17. Sperber, "Structure – Process – Trust," 167–68.

flict in the church, let alone society? Could we see conflict as a spiritual discipline in the community that can evolve into new ways of being the body of Christ? Or are we prone to seek comfort in silence, even if it perpetuates harm and division?[18] Buzz... buzz... again we are engaging the Gadfly.

One of the keys to creating a healthy space—in person, online, or hybrid—for participatory proclamation is to distinguish between debate and dialogue. Here, we may find ourselves resisting the Gadfly of social media (X, formerly known as Twitter in particular) where it seems every post is a *debate against* someone or something. A new media homilecclesiology invites Christians to practice *dialogue* instead, which does not avoid conflict and disagreement but does not dehumanize the people in the discussion, so that we all come to the table open to touch and transformation rather than closed-fisted and looking to win an argument.

Wesley Allen distinguishes between dialogue and debate for his conversational homiletic. At the root of his distinction is the posture of the partners in the event of a communicative encounter. One who enters the communication event with a certainty that is closed off from the possibility of conversion will be a grasping, violent force in the conversation. It only takes one grasping posture to shift the whole conversation from dialogue to debate. Allen continues by contrasting dialogue and debate: [19]

Table 1 Dialogue Compared to Debate	
Dialogue	Debate
Collaborative. Two or more sides work together toward common understanding.	Oppositional. Two sides oppose one another and attempt to prove one another wrong.
One listens to the other side(s) in order to understand, find meaning, and find agreement.	One listens to the other side in order to find flaws and to counter its argument.
Enlarges and possibly changes a participant's point of view.	Affirms a participant's own point of view.
Reveals assumptions for reevaluation.	Defends assumptions as truth.
Creates an open-ended attitude: an openness to being wrong and an openness to change.	Creates a close-minded attitude, and a determination to be right.

---

18. Moiso, "Standing in the Breach."
19. Allen, *Homiletic of All Believers*, 21–22.

Involves a real concern for the other person and seeks not to alienate or offend.	Involves countering the other position without focusing on feelings or relationships and often belittles or deprecates the other person.
Remains open-ended.	Implies a conclusion.

Dialogue is the posture and environment this book seeks to cultivate around preaching. The pastor-host and community of co-moderators will make and keep these expectations clear before the gathering. They will not hesitate to protect someone. Protection of an individual's rights to speak from their experience. Protection of the group dynamic from a climate of debate. Protection may even involve a subject in the sacred text who is being insensitively represented in the preaching. Protection also requires a layer of awareness of power dynamics in a community. Who has more power in this community, and so may need to be invited to not speak first or dominate the conversation? Whose voice is historically censored in this space and may need an invitation to share? Those superhuman powers of emotional intelligence and intercultural competence from chapter 5 will be necessary. New media preaching embodies a spirituality of holy dialogue with God and one another as we gather around a theme/text from Scripture.

Today's technoculture claims that conflict is an excuse to drop out of a community and find another that thinks just like us. But conflict can be the beginning of transformation, an opportunity to allow the Holy Spirit to deepen our connections to one another, God, and the pain of the world. Pastors and congregants who take up this posture in preaching—be it in the sanctuary or online—will cultivate and live.

Ambiguous Authorities: Democratization of News and Information

> The new Christian leader is a host, not an authority who dispenses settled truths, wise words, and the sole path to salvation . . . Today, the leaders who influence our faith and action are those who convene (or moderate or enable) the conversations that change our life . . . Christian leadership is about enabling significant community around the name of Jesus, wherever two or more are gathered in his name.[20]

---

20. Clayton, "Church After Google," paras. 39–40.

In chapter 4, we learned about the ambiguous authorities that emerge from social media technoculture. With smart devices in our hands that allow us to share, spread, and create information instantly, we have democratized power regarding who gets to have a voice in the public space. Autocracies scramble to control and censor social media so they can maintain the cultural storyline. In Web 3.0, mass media has truly given way to social media. Top-down, single-source media of the past maintained high barriers regarding what news and information are accurate and relevant to society. The monopoly on information perpetuated one-way lines of power that led to the press having control over the consumers of it. Low barriers to spreading and creating news and information mark participatory technoculture. Authorities emerge as the ones within this technoculture who make and maintain hubs of connection.

Preachers have always known that their central role is to be personally connected with God so that they may be stewards of the connection among others. The church has expected the ordained preacher to be anointed and appointed, to have a special connection with the Spirit of God, and to lead out of that connection. In the print-post-Gutenberg, top-down model of preaching, the preacher has been the gateway to God via special knowledge of Scripture and truth—a not-so-ambiguous authority.

The quote that opened this section is our clue to the role and authority of the pastor today. In a network(ed), post-Google model of preaching, the pastor's role is to create a hospitable commons where people feel the lure to connect with God and one another. After Google, the role of the preacher is the host or moderator who convenes encounters with the living Word of God. This enables the community to foster significant connections in the name of Jesus. In other words, we do not need a preacher to be Siri, Google, ChatGPT, or Alexa, dispensing information about God. The new media preacher is a host who gathers the community around Jesus for life-changing conversations wherein truths are discovered over time.

If the pastor's role in preaching shifts into the role of host or moderator, what precisely is the pastor hosting and moderating, preaching-wise? To answer this question, let us turn again to Priya Parker, author of *The Art of Gathering: How We Meet and Why it Matters*. Parker's description of "generous authority" in the role of host is one that the church can learn from.

Parker disdainfully explains, "A ubiquitous strain of twenty-first-century culture is infecting our gatherings: being chill. The desire to host while being noninvasive."²¹ The host in this scenario simply tells people to come over anytime within a window, doesn't carry through a purpose for the gathering (including who is and is not on the invite list), and then does not guide people during the event—not helping make connections, share in group activity, or think through a good ending to the time shared together.

Why is chill behavior from a host so revolting to Parker? Because the host is supposed to be the one who always has the *why*—the purpose—of the gathering in their mind so that it informs and forms their interactions with guests. When the host does not use the power and authority that they already have to call the gathering to order in the first place, guests may feel awkward and passive, checking their watches and waiting for the appropriate time to bail. Meanwhile, other guests might see the chance to assert their power and take over hosting duties instead.

Parker suggests that hosting a gathering is a responsibility that should not be taken lightly. A chill host might prioritize their own comfort and avoid making difficult decisions or engaging in the necessary work to create a meaningful experience for their guests. In doing so, they might inadvertently undermine the purpose and potential impact of the gathering.

Parker's critique of the host is applicable beyond conversational preaching. Monological preaching can sometimes be done by a chill host who does not use their pastoral power to carry a theme through. The sermon might not be written in conversation with the liturgy, the liturgical season, or the current worship series. The preacher might not have a focused sermon—just scattered ideas that do not help the listener connect with Scripture as a living word for their lives. Desiring to be noninvasive, the chill host preacher might not touch on current events that could make the listener uncomfortable, so the sermon seems to come from no time into a congregation void of pressing worries or concerns about life. This is preaching that is out of touch with God, neighbor, and self. It is a preaching of self-soothing meant not to offend or move or motivate anyone to connect the Living Word with a life lived Monday to Friday.

Of course, there is another pole on the spectrum of hosting: the host who exerts too much power over their guests. This host controls every aspect of the gathering and does not hold space for guests to practice any autonomy. Parker cautions, "If you are going to hold your guests captive, you had better do it well."²² Guests could reject the authority of the host and

21. Parker, *Gathering*, 73.
22. Parker, *Gathering*, 105.

abandon the aims of the gathering to form their own assembly, or abandon this one. Guests also might not make any meaningful connections with each other because all energy is focused on the host-to-guest relationship. When the host leaves center stage, the guests aren't sure how to connect and collaborate with one another.

In some ways, this authoritarian form of hosting is a lot like Palmer's mythical objectivism or Clayton's description of theology after Gutenberg. This host overuses their power to grasp and control outcomes. Fear is often the reason for this posture. Parker says, "The host most likely to succumb to ungenerous authority is the one who fears losing control. It is in the obsession with knowing how events will play out that we often make them go poorly . . . for the sake of calming ourselves."[23] What is interesting to note here is that fear is also present in the chill host's posture. The chill host fears being invasive or offensive, so their posture becomes one of *abandon*. The authoritarian host fears loss of control and so their posture becomes one of *grasping*. Both desire their own comfort more than desiring to orchestrate *touch*—a purposeful gathering with the guests' needs, wants, and potential in mind.

"So as a host," Parker asks, "how do you get your power right? How do you not abandon your guests while ensuring that your power serves them?"[24] By practicing what Parker calls generous authority. Parker describes the activities of generous authority as revolving around three verbs: "protecting, equalizing, connecting" those in the gathering.[25] These verbs are essential to design a space for people to gather in ways that enable mutual touch so truths are disclosed.

Pastors as hosts are not separate from what is taking place; they are themselves participants. They need to show up as humans with opinions and experiences in the gathering. The pastor practices what Ruth Cohn calls "participative leadership"—keeping in touch with the group and the shared thematic concern. In TCI, the moderator is not standing outside of the interaction and is not the star of the show. In other words, the pastor operates in between the poles of chill and authoritarian host as described by Parker. Cohn goes on to say about participative leadership that leaders are only secondarily functioning to maintain the dynamics "between the

---

23. Parker, *Gathering*, 103.
24. Parker, *Gathering*, 106.
25. Parker, *Gathering*, 95.

A New Media Homilecclesiology

I, the We, the It, and their connections to the Globe."[26] Primarily, they are humans interacting with fellow humans beings. To not participate or only manage the group dynamics is to erase the humanity of the host. As Cohn said,

> It is my responsibility not to extract myself from the leadership function—from myself, from the group, or from the theme. I feel, I think, I am bothered, I am calm, I am apathetic, I am impassioned—however I may feel at that moment. I do not want to remove myself from things, but rather, I want to direct my attention to you and support the theme. I am optimally (not maximally!) transparent to you.[27]

I will not have time to dive deeply into the concerns named in chapter 5 about generative AI here. However, chatbots are the ultimate ambiguous authority. They cannot practice participative leadership because they are not primarily human beings with consciousness, experience, and embodied wisdom. Their humanity is a costume, and sadly, some people do not have the media literacy to understand that they are not communicating with a real human being who is lovingly made by God when they are interacting with AI.

Moving at the Speed of the Feed: Time and the Social Media

Finally, we engage the Gadfly of time in this technocultural landscape. This section will be brief, as the practices in the final chapter model ways to shift into timely homiletical engagement through social media. Engaging the Gadfly on this theme comes down to one question: What if preachers prepared the message out loud and collaboratively through social media?

Social media creates opportunities for the pastor to cultivate the sermon collaboratively and in time with others in their network throughout the week. A pastor might literally "go live" on Facebook or Instagram to share their initial responses to the Scripture for Sunday. They might also offer prompts to their network and anticipate responses that will shape the sermon.

In chapter 4, we also discussed the desire to hear responses from authorities the moment news breaks. I am not suggesting that pastors need

---

26. Hinter, Middelkoop, and Wolf-Hollander, "Participative Leadership," 171.
27. Hinter, Middelkoop, and Wolf-Hollander, "Participative Leadership," 172.

to keep their eyes on the twenty-four-hour news cycle. But I suggest that pastors discern when breaking news is close to their congregation and be ready to offer a brief response, prayer, or action on social media. Your voice and presence are needed before Sunday's announcements, pastoral prayer, or sermon.

Another practice I will describe in the last chapter relates to shortening attention spans. Instead of posting the twenty- to forty-minute sermon on Sunday afternoon or Monday, think about ways to break the sermon into digestible pieces to disperse throughout the week on the church's social media. How many reels or stories can one sermon hold? And if people are drifting off in our messages (which *never* happens to me when I am preaching nor when I am listening to sermons), how might they have another chance to hear the message, this time in the setting of their feed or stories in the middle of the workday?

Reimagining and repurposing the monological sermon for social media is a way to remain in touch with the community throughout their week in X-reality. In little two-minute clips, we can invite the person scrolling in their feed to pause and pay attention to the presence of God. We can remind them that they are somebody who is part of the body of Christ.

I will end this section on time with an interesting, subversive movement online known as "digital gardening." This practice is well documented in online/social media/Web 3.0 culture, beginning with Mike Caulfield's 2015 keynote "The Garden and the Stream: A Technopastoral."[28] It's a posture that resists print media impressions; once I post something, it is a complete and final thought. It also resists the stream or feed of social media in which ideas are stated but cannot be deepened and developed because it is here today, gone tomorrow. Digital gardeners articulate their budding ideas openly, the ones that they've come back to again and again that are finally bearing fruit, and they show people how to think deeply on a subject over time. You can see an example of this practice on Maggie Appleton's website, "The Garden."[29] Each post has a date on which it was "planted" and when it was last "tended" to after considering new information and experience. Digital gardening is something more preachers could do with their congregations in X-reality, not to be an influencer receiving likes but to be an influencer inviting others into thoughtfulness, reflection, and imagination.

28. Caulfield, "Technopastoral."
29. Appleton, "Garden."

A New Media Homilecclesiology

CONCLUSION

Touch does not rely upon the most basic sensation of skin-to-skin contact, though it does include that. Touch is recognized as a full-body sensation of encountering another in mutually affirming ways. It means there is enough space in the encounter for my individuality not to be overridden by another's. This is how God touches creation, after all. We are not puppets pulled by God's strings, as much as it might ease some of our anxiety to relinquish control to a sovereign power. God does not grasp. God does not let go. Rather, God gently offers us direction, invites us to be in touch, and mourns each moment we do not take God up on that offer without turning that open hand into a fist. This is where sin enters the picture: in our resistance to vulnerable and tender relationships with God and others.

For centuries in the Protestant church, the body of Christ network has been given fewer and fewer opportunities to "fire together and wire together." This is part of a phrase inspired by Donald Hebb, a neuropsychologist, in 1949. The full phrase, coined by Carla Shatz, is "neurons that fire together, wire together," meaning paths in the brain are formed and strengthened through repeated interaction. Scientists like Suzanne Simard notice a similar phenomenon in the ecosystem of the forests of British Columbia, describing how vital those fungal connections in the soil are for the ecosystem's health. And in Ephesians, we are reminded of Jesus' design for the Way to be based on gatherings of people woven together through the power of the Holy Spirit. *Henotes:* We need each other.

From Parker Palmer and Phillip Clayton's models mentioned earlier, we can describe the pastor-as-host as one who cultivates an environment for truths to emerge through community interaction. The pastor exercises generous authority, protecting, equalizing, and connecting the gathering to God, neighbor, and self through proclamation. It takes skill and know-how to live into this why for a gathering, because most pastors have been taught—in seminary and through worship—to be solely responsible for delivering a message to connect to people (one-to-many). However, the host is not the sole messenger in an event. Now the pastor is empowering many-to-many connections.

At the same time, the congregation needs to see themselves as co-moderators of the gathering who protect, equalize, and foster connection between each other and the living Word. The ways we have designed worship for centuries have led to chill guests who will need some encouragement to participate in proclamation, be it on social media, in a midweek gathering, or live in the sermon event. A new media homilecclesiology invites the laity to see themselves as co-moderators of communal gathering around the Word.

In an age when we are asked on a daily basis to jump through hoops to confirm our humanity online, this approach to preaching does indeed confirm and affirm our humanity. We will hear from one another and be inspired, surprised, uncomfortable, angry, curious . . . and instead of turning away, we will learn how to stay in touch with each other as we all seek to be in touch with the Holy Three in One.

If you feel overwhelmed by these shifts—from preacher as expert to preacher as host; from pastor as master of divinity to pastor as moderator or midwife of divinity—then take heart. I mean this literally! Take heart, and have courage. This is the message of Parker Palmer's book on teaching, which shifts from the expert/amateur foundation to one in rooted in communities of truth. We will need courage, both as pastors and laity, when we turn toward each other more frequently and allow ourselves to be in touch with one another's joys, sorrows, anger, confusion, agony, doubt, and delight. Perfect love casts out fear not rooted in awe of God. Love in action protects, equalizes, and connects the body within its ecosystem. We act as Christ acted, love incarnate, as we explore a new media homiletic in which many voices speak, and ears listen (including the pastor's).

The preaching that takes place among a twenty-first-century priesthood of all believers in a framework of touch will only go as deep as the soul-climate of the participants. It has always been the case that a preacher preaches out of who they are. Preachers are not merely sharing information about God; they are, with their very presence, reflecting their relationship with/in God. The onus is on us to be better antennae for God in a saturated, distracted, and distanced world. Not everyone listens for God's whisper above the noise of this world. We will need to. As Marjorie Suchocki repeatedly says in her theology of preaching from a process theological perspective, "Because the revealed word of God in Jesus Christ is a historical word, given in time, preaching is absolutely required as the extension of God's incarnation in Christ across history."[185] Homilecclesiology—which calls for a preaching priesthood of all believers—calls for deepened spirituality within the whole church universal. Because God is in the community of believers, and truth emerges from our interactions over time.

Though we may have the best intentions of being co-conspirators with God, there is also in human nature a possibility for sinful and tragic choices

A New Media Homilecclesiology

to be made, at times intentionally and at other times unintentionally. We do not always make decisions without pausing, giving time and space to listen to God's whisper and lure. We can be reactive out of selfish and self-centered (narrow) spaces of our soul and put our (I/self) ahead of others to the extent of harm. It is often the case that woundedness leads to desperate grasping for and of an other. In some cases, benign differences tragically drift into becoming malignant conflicts. A posture of touch—modeled after the incarnation— encourages patience, listening, and compassionate awareness of the many wounds present in online and in-person discourse.

Perhaps our stumbling block to this profoundly relational vision for the priesthood of all believers and ministry to the living Word is that it calls for the long, slow work of remaining connected to people and connecting people to the living Word of God. We may prefer to preach (and receive) a message that is perfected, completed, and spoken with the power to grasp us firmly and without ambiguity. It is difficult to cultivate the patience and persistence to be in touch with each other and with the whisper of God and to wait and work together for truth to emerge. At times, leaders seek to control wayward people, those who challenge their vision of the future, and then they fall into grasping. At other times, the laity grows weary in the chaos of violence, debate, and apathy of our world and falls into grasping by seeking a charismatic figure to solve the problem for them, to make and fulfill a promise that truth as they deliver it guarantees a tragedy-free life. We fragile human beings fall into grasping and out of mutual connection in various ways at various times.

A new media homilecclesiology emphasizes building trust and perhaps authority through convening a community around the living Word. Homilecclesiological authority is relational in nature. It is also kenotic, requiring the refusal to assume power-over, and the cultivation of creativity and pastoral sensitivity. In homilecclesiology, we do not persuade and manipulate or broadcast and sell the gospel. Rather, we seek to make connections in life between tragedy and hope, mundane and sacred. In sum, the aim of preaching in homilecclesiology is not to grasp the audience with our message of truth. Rather, truth is understood like Palmer's pedagogical approach in *The Courage to Teach*: "an eternal conversation about things that matter, conducted with passion and discipline."[30]

In homilecclesiology, we do not use technology to broadcast truth as a static and timeless statement that is one size fits all, and that begins and

---

30. Palmer, *Courage to Teach*, 106.

ends with the preacher. That is certainly still done by broadcast preachers (or influencers) under the guise of the latest technologies. Though technologies make it possible for us to broadcast gospel and amplify our presence in ways unimagined before, homilecclesiology—a posture that is not rooted in technoculture yet open to engage and inform it—reminds us that such a goal is not fitting to the work of allowing the gospel to emerge through dialogue and mutuality over time.

CONVERSATION PROMPTS

1. What does it mean for you to experience touch in the sermon?
2. Which of Parker Palmer's figures most reflects the design of your worship service? Does the design enable your community's why for preaching and worship? How?
3. Reflect on your experience being hosted by someone. Can you think of examples of a chill host? Authoritarian? Someone who practiced generous authority as a host? How might those experiences shape your community's preaching practice?
4. Review the section comparing dialogue and debate from Wesley Allen. Which of these points most resonates with you, and why? Which point, if any, made you feel uncomfortable and why?
5. As we move to the last chapter on practice, notice how you feel about these invitations to engage the Gadfly and shift into more participatory preaching. What might these feelings communicate?

7

Reflective Preaching Practice for a Digital Age

"The folks participating in online church are by no means exclusively kids, youth, or twenty-somethings. The people who call Koinonia Congregational Church their spiritual home are young, old, black and white, American and European, gay and straight, and representing a spectrum of differently-abled bodies. One parishioner who has worshipped at Koinonia for nearly two years is a grandmother who lives alone and has experienced more than forty surgical procedures. Though homebound, she finds solace in a living Christian community that daily prays with her, visits with her, and worries about her when she is not around. One young woman, a lesbian living in a small southern community, came to Koinonia with deep wounds inflicted by her home congregation. Finding a church in her hometown was hard. In our church, she has found love and acceptance. Here, she has found a deep connection with God and peace with herself." —Kimberly Knight[1]

REFLECTIVE PREACHING AFTER COVID

When most congregations took preaching online in 2020, they transferred a print/broadcast why and how of preaching into a new technoculture. But

---

1. Knight, "Sacred Space," para. 14.

before COVID, innovative pastors had been forming new media congregations whose preaching praxis and ecclesiology reflected the shifts taking place:

- Lower hierarchical boundaries.
- Greater participation, many-to-many instead of one-to-many.
- Network and web-shaped communal structures instead of top-down.
- A welcome space for Christians to connect who felt disconnected from traditional, print technoculture churches.

An example of this sort of BC (before COVID) gathering was the Koinonia Congregational Church. You encountered them in the quote from pastor Kimberly Knight above. Koinonia gathered in Second Life, an online video game that started in 2003. The game is not fully scripted. However, people are allowed to create an avatar for themselves and interact with other people in co-constructed worlds. Robert Geraci, in his book *Virtually Sacred: Myth and Meaning in World of Warcraft and Second Life*, describes the human actors who intentionally and imaginatively proposed another life for religion. In Second Life, there is agility instead of religious fragility. Here, they can "build churches, temples . . . offer theologies or design new practices,"[2] which is precisely what Kimberly Knight did with the Koinonia community. Through co-creation, a clear why for gathering, a host pastor who helped moderate the environment, diverse people gathered around the living Word and encountered God.

These past five years have been challenging, and your community's ability to adapt and evolve in these circumstances is commendable. Depending on how long your community gathered exclusively through new platforms during the pandemic, your preaching may have changed in response to dwelling in the new ecosystem, with:

- Shorter monologue sermons.
- Hosts in chat spaces to engage in conversations.
- Multimedia for Scripture, sermon, songs—not just word-based.

Rather than go back to preaching as usual, I invite you to consider incarnational ways of shifting the preaching practices that are responsive to shifts

---

2. Geraci, *Virtually Sacred*, 166.

in technoculture. Reflect and learn from what the Gadfly has revealed so far. Here are a few lessons we've learned along the way that the Gadfly wants:

- Imagine a shift from broadcast preaching to socially mediated proclamation.
- To challenge "spectatoritis" and the "monological illusion" not only in online and social media spaces but in the analog space as well.
- To remind you that technology is not neutral . . . it is having an impact on our being/becoming.
- To amplify human-to-human interactions amid this epidemic of loneliness.
- To become a prompt engineer who helps invite others to engage with Scripture.

These shifts in preaching after Google are not zoned solely for online and hybrid preaching. Even conventional churches that will not sell their building and design a virtual space for worship can reimagine preaching that responds to the Gadfly.

How do we live in networked ways of becoming the body of Christ? How can we, through preaching, curate a sense of communal belonging and responsibility for creation? How can we adapt what we learned in the previous chapter about the posture of the preacher as host, the tenets of Ruth Cohn's Theme Centered Interaction (TCI), and Redditors into practice today?

ENGAGING THE GADFLY IN THE ANALOG CHURCH

We begin our journey into preaching practices with those of you who hardly dabble in streaming or recording the worship service on Sunday and do not curate a specifically online worship service later. You are the analog church.

What do I mean by analog? In this case, analog is an adjective that distinguishes itself from digital. Jay Y. Kim applies this distinction to the church in *Analog Church: Why We Need Real People, Places, and Things in the Digital Age*. In short, Kim invites congregations to remain analog in a sea change of churches going digital to be relevant.

You might be an analog congregation if (cue Jeff Foxworthy impersonation):

- The sermon has a tidy spot within a fifty- to ninety-minute worship service.
- The length of the monologue falls between twelve and forty-five minutes.
- The location for preaching tends to be the pulpit, or stage, or a music stand.
- The location for the rest of the congregation is arranged so that all eyes are on the preacher and folks can sit comfortably for the majority of the service.
- The sermon flows one way and rarely is anyone invited to interrupt the sermon with their thoughts beyond *amen, okay preacher, go ahead and say it,* or if you are struggling, *Lord help them!*
- You do not have any cameras in the sanctuary. No livestream, no recording to post later.
- Or you do have a camera whose only purpose is to project the image of the preacher or worship leaders onto screens inside the building.

As the world goes digital, Kim invites the church to stay analog, which, in his understanding, is characterized by meeting together for worship and community "in real time and real space."[3] In other words, Kim sets up a binary world in which digital worship and community is not real. In contrast, analog (in person, in the building) worship and community is really real.

I am sure by now you can guess that I do not believe that analog church—in-person, synchronous worship—is more real than digital church. After all, the analog church was indeed greatly shaped by the technological changes of the print age, for good and for bad. Yet, the term can still help us describe the congregation that is not yet integrating livestreaming, recordings, hybrid, or other platforms for assembling a worship community.

Kim overlooks some aspects of digital technoculture that may not be out of line with Christian worship traditions: participation, the work of the people, testimony, mediating the gospel with the tools at our fingertips, welcoming the outcast, and amplifying the presence of the Spirit are all possible in digital spaces and through digital culture in the analog space. Engaging the Gadfly means taking part in the transformation not by ignoring the technoculture but by intentionally showing up in the world differently. As James K. A. Smith said in an interview on cultural liturgies at the Yale

3. Kim, *Analog*, 11.

Reflective Preaching Practice for a Digital Age

Youth Ministry Institute, we cannot say to the culture we swim in, forget you; I am swimming elsewhere![4] Rather, we need to teach our community about the water we swim in (digital technoculture) and encourage them to "swim differently" within it to promote flourishing in this context. This is our calling as congregations. Preaching is only one piece of the puzzle we are putting together to swim differently in these digital waters.

While this new media homilecclesiology in its fullness allows for dialogue *in* the sermon event, it can still offer sermon planning and delivery guides for the analog pulpit preacher and congregation. Any of the forms in the rest of the chapter can be applied to an analog church. A useful guide remains John S. McClure's *The Roundtable Pulpit: Where Leadership and Preaching Meet.* Published in 1995, this book was ahead of its time, anticipating the shifts taking place in technoculture. Explore how to prepare, deliver, and dialogue as a church in technocultural shift. Keep before you the lessons from part one as we explore ways to stretch into engagement with the gadfly of digital technoculture:

- Preachers are more than Alexa/Siri/Google/chatbots programmed for God/theology.
- Preaching is more than the delivery of information into the minds of the congregation.[5]
- The congregation's spiritual growth will be improved by cross-pollinating the theme-centered interaction of the preacher's message through dialogue—between the preacher and the people and between the people in the pew.

The analog church, as Jay Kim describes it, does not contain analog people (surely there are rare exceptions to that rule). Our current technoculture is still shaping them in the ways they think, process, communicate, and relate to one another. Some of those influences should indeed be resisted with a "Holy No" to say Yes to the life-giving practices of Christianity. Individualism, loneliness, polarization, and dehumanization of any kind deserve a holy no from the church. We can live into this no by stretching into more participatory preaching praxis.

---

4. Yale Youth Ministry Institute, *Dr. James K. A. Smith.*

5. For more on preaching in ways that are not just for the transmission of information, read Voelz, *Preaching to Teach.*

Engaging the Gadfly

DIGITAL PRACTICES OF A NEW MEDIA HOMILECCLESIOLOGY

A congregation can take many adventures in living out a new media homilecclesiology. While particular platforms may come and go, the shifts will endure into the emerging generations of humans who gather as a church. Engaging some or all of the following practices will stretch the church into interactive preaching and away from performative practices that rely on one expert to entertain a church audience.

Before I discuss four examples of applying the new media homilecclesiology of touch to preaching, I want to highlight three conversation partners. The first partner is a resource that suits a congregational conversation, and the other two are exclusively written for the pastor.

Read Meredith Gould's *The Social Media Gospel: Sharing the Good News in New Ways* for a more direct, hands-on explanation of social media and its potential for sharing the gospel. This book covers the dominant platforms one can engage and explains basic terminology to a broad audience. It will help your congregation discern which platforms are best suited for your context, assets, and mission. The book also offers a set-by-step guide for creating a platform for the church. Finally, Gould helps the congregation cultivate social media policy, a must for the digital age.

Now for the resources more focused on the pastor and their preaching practice. First, explore Rob O'Lynn's *Digital Jazz: Preaching, Media, and Technology* for tips and tricks on how a preacher can enhance their preaching through creative engagement with new technologies. This guide moves beyond preaching into topics of administration and pastoral care with technological tools. O'Lynn also offers a simple strategy for avoiding plagiarism. Finally, for an overview of various ways exclusively online preaching can take place, read Sunguu A. Yang's *Digital Homiletics: The Theology and Practice of Online Preaching*. He summarizes the various styles of online preaching. This book is also one for the pastor/preacher to reflect on the identity cultivated through the style of online preaching they practice and merits, locations, times, and designs for each style.

Broadly speaking, the process for planning any type of dialogical-digital preaching involves three actions: 1) Decide what theme/text we will focus on this week. Begin by looking back and ahead, always connected to the whole preaching ministry; 2) Start to share the homiletical process with your network; 3) Come up with three levels of prompts for the feedforward and/or in-person dialogical sermon.

Model One: escalate slowly toward a personal question

1. A prompt about the text that stirs up people's curiosity about the ancient context, words, and places (a posture of touch and humanization toward historical others).
2. A prompt about God/Spirit/Jesus in the world of the text (a posture of touch and curiosity toward theological others).
3. A prompt about us, the implications of the text's meaning for our time and place (a posture of touch and humanization toward each other and our world).

Model Two: use "I, We, It" prompts (TCI, Ruth Cohn)

1. A prompt that helps the individual reflect on what they see/feel/notice in the text or about the sermon theme/topic (I).
2. A prompt to invite individuals to read and respond to others in the chain/chat with gratitude and curiosity (We).
3. A prompt to consider how the theme might stir up our action in our time and place (It).

Now, let's dive into four examples of a congregation practicing a new media homilecclesiology!

Example One: Sermon Preparation in X-Reality

There are so many ways for preachers to practice preparing the sermon out loud through social media. We just need to break the habit of perfectionism that leads many of us not to share or say anything about what we preach on Sunday until Sunday arrives and the sermon is completed. Or you may have a procrastination issue, and the sermon is put together Saturday night or Sunday morning. Whatever the case may be, you, as the preacher, may be assisted and inspired by the interactions that take place through social media as you share your sermon process with the network.

I always tell my students that the first step in inviting participation in the sermon process is to take the time to plan out sermon series at least six months in advance. You can practice this if you are a lectionary preacher or a series thematic preacher. I always recommend that each series or season for preaching last somewhere between four and six weeks. This series might correspond to the liturgical year or to the secular year, such as seasons of summer and back to school or a hybrid of both. Whatever the case may be, it's easier for us to have a sense of flow and conversation about the preaching ministry when we are doing the long-term visioning and not just sprinting week to week and short-term preaching.

In this way, you are like the moderator of a subreddit who is taking responsibility for the theme-centered interactions that will take place within your gathering over time and now you are also ready to receive feedback and feedforward from your community as you share what the upcoming series will be and even give a preview of what each week might address through Scripture or topically or both. Using a resource like Rob O'Lynn's *Digital Jazz*, you can create a social media strategy. This strategy will include creating a centering image for the series that can be used to not only promote or broadcast what the series will be about but to signal to people in the congregation and in the network that discussion is taking place around this theme.

Next, we can consider what an ordinary preacher's week looks like. Some preachers finish on Sunday, and after that holy pastor nap, they begin to think about next week and what the connection will be from that day's sermon to the sermon that will be preached the following week. Instead of only taking down notes in a memo on your phone or holding it in your head or jotting it down on a piece of paper, what if you shared these hints and glimpses toward the next Sunday with your congregational network?

On Monday and Tuesday of the preacher's week, we typically sit with the Scripture or Scriptures for the coming Sunday. I always encourage my students not to rush to commentaries in this precious moment of holy listening and discernment of what the Holy Spirit is guiding the pastor to notice in this text for their people in this time and place. But the pastor does not have to rely on holy imagination alone. Through social media, the pastor can assemble a round table conversation with the Scripture ahead of Sunday. Who are the people you would like to see at this round table? Suppose you are looking for responses from people who do not go to your church or would not consider themselves Christian. In that case, you want to make sure that you are going live on a social media platform like TikTok or Instagram and Facebook, depending on your settings that allow for public presence. In this case, it might be beneficial for the pastor to go live on their personal profile instead of the church's, if their goal is to connect with folks outside the assembly.

But if you would like your round table to be focused on the people in your congregation, then I suggest you go live from or through the church's social media platforms. One of the things I love about this practice is that it can be a bridge of relationship-building between people who mostly attend worship online and people who participate in the building. If you host a round table that is accessible to both, then you can start to facilitate those many-to-many connections that result in deeper communities and combat loneliness, isolationism, and fear of the other. A boundaried space—one that is created by invitation and not broadcast to the public—like Zoom allows the community not just to see the names and profile pictures of each other but also to get to see the faces and hear the voices of the participants at the round table.

Whichever method you choose, I always tell my students that if this is something they want to implement in their ministry, it is best to establish a regular time and day for this practice. It might take a few weeks or months before congregants are clued in to your livestream. Still, once they know you are going live on Instagram or Facebook, they may be more inclined to join the conversation and share their reflections with you on those early days of sermon preparation.

If going live intimidates you, you can also be a prompt engineer by creating posts on social media. These posts could engage once again the anchor image for the sermon series or season, the Scripture gathered around on Sunday, and prompts for reflection. You can encourage the gathering to comment on the prompts and share their stories related to the theme ahead of the sermon.

Responses do not only have to be text-based comments on Facebook or Instagram. A platform like TikTok allows you to encourage congregants to create a stitch or a duet that responds to the pastor's initial seed for the sermon. If you are concerned about privacy and ensuring that the shy soul feels safe to show up in conversation, then your community can always decide to create a private Facebook group for these conversations that are more intimate and are housed within a more public presence on social media. You could also use platforms educators use, like Padlet, that require a join code and are extremely user-friendly spaces for hosting topical conversations in the community through the camera and voice instead of being text-based alone.

These suggested approaches to sermonic feedforward in the digital age can be practiced whether the sermon on Sunday will be a traditional monologue or a conversational sermon. Either way, the preacher as host empowers the congregation to engage with holy Scriptures and participate more fully because they can prepare themselves for the sermonic event in advance. The preacher is given a chance to grow in their cultivation of the sermon because of the interactions that are taking place through social media.

Remember the advice from the previous chapter. How can the congregation partner with the preacher as host to cultivate a space where everyone feels like they can share their testimony, their witness, and their experience without being threatened or debated? Many social media groups and gatherings create a covenant pinned to the top of the page that offers ethical guidelines for how and why the community will interact with each other. Creating this sort of social media covenant or policy can be a generative process for a congregation to engage the Gadfly of social media theologically.

My task in this book will not be to help your congregation decide which social media platforms to engage in and why. As a reminder, Meredith Gould's *The Social Media Gospel* is an excellent resource if you are in the early stages of cultivating a social media presence for your congregation. However, I will say that it is better for a church that wants to engage the Gadfly to do so through a Facebook page or a Facebook group that belongs to the body of the congregation. I prefer this method to relying upon the pastor's social media profile for these conversations and interactions. Depending upon your tradition, the pastor may only be at the congregation for four years or even less. The social media ministry of the church will not endure if it relies upon the pastor's leadership and personality alone.

Example Two: Sermon Feedback in X-Reality

The previous section on sermon feedforward lays the groundwork for sermon feedback and X-reality. As I share with all the pastors that I coach and the students I teach, I am introducing you to many practices in this chapter, but I do not expect any pastor or congregation to take up all of them. After you've read through all these examples, you will have a sense of what fits your congregation's why and personality best. For some, feedforward that shapes the sermon may be of utmost importance. For others, empowering the congregation to embody the sermon from Sunday, Monday through Saturday, will be of the utmost importance. This is what I mean by sermon feedback.

Sermon feedback through X-reality does not involve asking the congregation whether they liked the sermon. Instead, it's finding ways to engage social media to help the message on Sunday be in dialogue with their ordinary lives. We know that attention spans are not what they used to be in this digital age. It can be hard for any attentive congregant to hear the fullness of a twenty- or forty-minute sermon on Sunday. Sharing snippets of the message preached on Sunday on social media throughout the week allows the congregant to interact with the message in the complexity of their lives. When they are invited to share their responses and reflections on the sermon through social media, we once again increase the many-to-many connections within the congregation by gathering around the living word of God.

Sometimes, I see pastors and congregations who think that reposting a clip of the whole sermon that was livestreamed or recorded on Sunday on social media or YouTube is enough to foster engagement with this sermon throughout the week. We might have the occasional congregant who wants to rewatch or relisten to the entirety of the sermon on their lunch break or on a run, etc. But when it comes to interacting with the congregation and creating possibilities for people not yet involved in the congregation to glean insight and wisdom through the sermon, the best approach is to lift one- to three-and-a-half-minute-long snippets of the Sunday sermon. Snippets of the longer sermon that are at most a minute and a half long can easily capture the attention of the congregant or the seeker who is in scroll mode or story mode on their smartphones throughout the week. You always have the option of including a link to the full sermon on the reel or story. If the snippet is intriguing enough to the person who's engaging it on social media they have the option to click on the link and hear the whole sermon. But the snippet should be a cohesive enough piece of theological insight like it can stand alone without hearing the whole sermon.

When I coach pastors, they often ask how they can find a minute-and-a-half snippet of their sermons to post on social media channels. My preferred method is to utilize a platform for podcasting called Descript. With Descript, you can upload an audio or video file in its entirety, and you will be shown a transcript of the file to use for editing purposes. By editing the text on Descript, you can create a segment of audio that you can share on social media channels. You can also clean up the audio file, removing any "ums," extended pauses, or other tics in the message. You also can utilize some free basic instrumental pieces of music that can go beneath the audio clip. This certainly is less time-consuming than listening to a twenty- or forty-minute sermon and finding the timestamp of the clips you want to share on social media.

Finally, you can also go live and host synchronous conversations midweek about the sermon. The pastor-host can create prompts that help the community remember what the implications for the sermon were on Sunday and reflect on how the message has rung true or not in their ordinary lives this week. Were there any moments of synchronicity inspired by the sermon? Did congregants make certain decisions and choices about their behaviors and actions because of the message on Sunday? This is an opportunity not just for the pastor alone to receive feedback on how the message is living within a congregant but again to facilitate many-to-many connections where the whole of the congregation and even people on the fringes of the network can hear in real time how the sermon is being lived incarnationally.

Questions for reflection on church social media presence

- Does your congregation have a social media presence?
- If so, are members of the congregation active on the congregation's page or platform? Why or why not?
- If you have multiple social media platforms for the church, do they all have the same avatar/profile picture, information, and contact information?
- Which of the suggested practices above feel achievable? Uncomfortable? Why?

Example Three: Hosting Dialogue in Livestream Preaching

After COVID closures, the data gathered by Barna painted a new portrait of what it looks like to participate in worship in the future, especially with younger generations:

Before the COVID-19 pandemic, the majority of church attendance happened exclusively in person. Today, that's only true for about half of churched adults. In fact, one in five (20%) is still primarily attending online, and one in four (26%) is mixing online and in-person worship. While in-person attendance is still reported by the plurality of churched adults, regardless of age, Millennial churched adults are most likely to have embraced hybrid options, with one in three attending both online and in person.[6]

This following section is for congregations that will continue to livestream the sermon from the building onto various platforms such as YouTube or Facebook Live. Hybrid preaching is where a great number of congregations in the United States live since March 2020. When I receive pre-workshop survey results from congregations, anywhere between 75 percent and 95 percent of them livestream Sunday worship and/or record the service and post it on YouTube or Vimeo later. But not all of these pastors and congregations are sure why they continue to livestream. Often, they share something along the lines of the following concerns:

- How can I effectively preach to both, simultaneously?
- Who is the who out there on the other end of the livestream?
- I struggle because I don't get any feedback from the congregation online. The lack of felt engagement and connection is challenging.
- How can I bring awareness and connection between the congregation in the building and the one online?

If the congregation determines that they commit to building up the church through hybrid preaching, then it is time to address these concerns with reflective practices. The first step (or, as my TheoTechnics colleague Samantha Potter would say, the third step after making sure the audio and video are clear) is to train moderators for the livestream experience intentionally. This includes greeters and gatherers of prayer concerns. However, specifically concerning the sermon, it involves moderating the chat.

What I mean by this is that on these livestreams, there is often a chat feature where the people participating in worship online can greet one another to shout "Amen" or have their own side conversations during the sermon. I often see congregations completely ignore these comments, at times unaware that people are posting in the chat. This is not an effective

---

6. Barna, "New Chapter in Millennial Church Attendance."

and reflective use of the chat. It is also not an example of hosting with generous authority. No chill hosts! If the stream is there, train a volunteer or volunteers to moderate and show hospitality. Is there anyone in your congregation (not the preacher in the pulpit) who would be interested in being an online ministry presence for this community?

Leaders in the congregation can also intentionally find ways to build connections between congregants who worship online and those who are in the building. These connections may not be facilitated through chat, an organic function of social media spaces but not a welcome practice in the pews. Anyone who has nudged a partner or whispered to someone in the pew during the sermon can probably sense the energy of those around them shifting into annoyance. Implementing practices in the previous sections of feedforward and/or feedback through social media can help close the gap between remote congregants and people in the building.

We need to imagine other ways to foster many-to-many connections in the congregation. I imagine new proposals will enter the conversation as we move into the middle of the twenty-first century. One suggestion for now is using live in-meeting polling apps to bridge the gap. Mentimeter is an example of a popular (and free) platform for interactive live polling. Open-ended responses can be visualized through word clouds. Or a poll could be created ahead of time with multiple-choice options, including one that allows folks to respond to prompts on a sliding scale. What is great about a platform like this is that anyone can contribute anonymously, and the gathering can visualize a sense of the gathering as a whole, not just in the building or online.

Example Four: Hosting Dialogue in Person or Online

In the following section, I will move from *"our congregation is pretty traditional and will not take a leap into dialogical sermons, but we might be okay with a little experimentation"* to *"we know the monologue form of proclamation is not drawing us into the living word as a community, so let's go all the way!"* Remember, there is no right or wrong way to apply homilecclesiology to the sermon event. Even if you begin and sit with the previous suggestions for engaging the Gadfly and increasing participation through the sermon process, then you are shifting into a more reflective, communal approach to preaching, which is the hope I have for you as you read this book and discuss it with others!

So, let's start with just an occasional pattern of dialogue and see where that adventure takes us.

Mode One: Shalom Sundays

Even though many people in our congregations engage in social media in some form or another throughout the week, we must recognize that many choose not to. If the only space for dialogical interaction with the sermon is digital spaces, we are leaving some out.

So why not bring the spirit of dialogue into the sermon event on Sunday for at least some of the time?

What if a Sunday between transitions in the calendar reflected the previous season and anticipation of the coming season through a panel or conversational sermon? Now, we really see an image of the host that is familiar to many of us across generations. On a Shalom Sunday, at the end of a sermon series, the pastor-host moderates a live conversation with a panel of congregants who have participated in the series.

For congregations that are curious about adding dialogical spaces into worship but are interested in making a partial switch from monological preaching, I suggest implementing an occasional end-of-sermon/worship series dialogical sermon on a Shalom Sunday. Shalom is a Hebrew word that means not only peace but wholeness. I was part of a congregation with Shalom Sundays on the fifth Sunday of every month, where the youth worshiped with the adults instead of in their classrooms. I am using Shalom Sunday to describe a Sunday when the sermon is a live response of selected congregation members to a sermon series. The pastor-host listens and offers no monologue on this day.

If you are part of a larger congregation, you could have the pastor host a panel of laity during the sermon moment. The pastor and leadership should choose folks who feel comfortable being up front and have been present throughout the sermon series. Selecting a diverse representation from the congregation is recommended—ages, duration of membership in the community, vocation . . . whatever diversity is in your location.

Apply the recommendations throughout this book and host from the beginning, and do not be chill as the facilitator of the proclamation. Set the scene and empower participants to preach from their valuable human experiences and perspectives. Remind the community of its guidelines for listening and engaging with diverse responses. To empower depth, share the prompts you want the panel to respond to ahead of time and be open to some pre-worship conversations. Ensure that each panelist gets the chance to respond to each question and one another. If you are searching for a prompt, begin with a question about what is historically called the function statement in homiletics:

> "Having heard the sermons in this series, what from these messages has impacted your life over the last few weeks? How?" The answers need not be grand and can relate more precisely to what they've observed about how they see/feel/think about God, neighbor, Jesus, church, the news, etc., considering this season or series.

Smaller congregations could skip the panel and move into dialogue as one group or around tables. As my friend and co-conspirator Teresa J. Stewart says, this is the small church advantage in a social media technoculture![7] If you sense that the whole congregation would be equipped for occasional dialogical preaching, transfer the principles of the panel to dialogue at tables or in pew sections between sermon series or seasons in the liturgical year. Depending on the pastor's comfort level, I recommend hosting a shared proclamation at a maximum of forty to fifty in the gathering (assuming they are all in the same space). You can look at the two conversational preaching models below to help frame the sermon event. If you have a hybrid congregation, work with a co-host who can collaborate to bring online dialogue into the in-person and vice versa. If you get beyond fifty in a gathering, then it is time to train co-hosts or table/pew/row/chat moderators for smaller groups of five to eight people.

The benefits of this practice are articulated in the previous chapter. We are strengthening communal bonds, shaping a congregation that learns how to listen to other perspectives without debating or fixing another person. A community of theologians is being cultivated as more people come into speech about their faith and understanding of God. Echo chambers are dissolved through hosted conversation.

Now, we can explore the possibility of dialogical preaching in the worship gathering. I will outline two models for you: 1) a model that keeps the framing of the theme from start to finish in the pastor's hands, and 2) a model that allows the multiple voices of the congregation to guide us into the next move of worship.

---

7. Stewart, *Small Church Advantage*.

Dan White Jr. created the first model, while the second is one I have developed over the years of preaching in dialogical worship communities. Both models open space and time for the congregation to share their witness and contribute to the proclamation from their experience and wisdom. The critical difference is that my model strives toward a postmodern form that doesn't turn back to the pastor's authority to offer a tidy (pastor-led and decided) conclusion.

Mode Two: Conversational Preaching (Two Options)

In *The Act of Dialogical Preaching: The Convergence of Conversation & Proclamation in Public Space*, Dan White Jr. proposes a form for hosting conversational sermons structured with four simple moves. First is the investigative move, followed by an expressive move, a collective move, and ending with a declarative move. White suggests that each of these moves last about ten minutes so that in approximately forty-five minutes, the sermon event begins and concludes in the Sunday worship service. Let's break down each of these moves briefly.

Option One: Dan White Jr.

Investigative

The first ten minutes of the model is a monological moment of preaching from the pastor. During these ten minutes, the preacher shares their exegesis of a passage. The preacher also brings the main point of the conversational sermon before the congregation. One of the strategies that White suggests is ending the exegetical moment with the preacher offering what he calls a "story-piece" that fits the main point.[8] White calls this a moment of contact between our story and the story of Scripture that is vital in inviting the congregation to also add their voices and stories to the sermon in the next move. White also offers physical cues for the preacher throughout the dialogical sermon that mirror their role in the sermonic moment. So, in this first move of investigation, the pastor is front and center, setting the scene for the dialogue. Because of this, White suggests that the preacher stands during this move.

---

8. White Jr., *Dialogical*, 15.

Wait Time

While it is not officially one of the four dialogical moves, White does suggest a wait time of silence lasting three minutes between the investigative move and the expressive move. He offers multiple reasons for introducing this time of silence, including a formational aspect of our technoculture, in which people are rarely invited to sit in silence. But this move also helps different types of thinkers. Not everyone in the congregation will be ready to dialogue immediately after hearing the preacher's setup and a story from a congregant. From this investigative move, White also suggests leaving the congregation with two questions to ponder in the silence. The first question is, "Where is there some conflict for you in this passage (what is the spirit disrupting)?" And the second question is, "Where is there some clarity for you in this passage (what is the spirit confirming)?"[9]

Expressive

According to White, "dialogical preaching includes not only the declarative but the discursive." Now, the congregation is invited to participate in the proclamation for approximately ten minutes. This is where the preacher moderator (my language) reminds the community of its commitment to dialogue and not debating each other or talking for too long so that many voices can express themselves.

As with the first move, White suggests posture for the preacher. Sit down on a stool. But make eye contact with each person who shares. Presumably, from his description, everyone in the congregation is invited to share their response to the prompts with the pastor. The model does not seem to suggest that these conversations are happening at separate tables.

Collective

After about ten minutes of sharing, the preacher stands up from the stool and invites the congregation to collect the "clarities and conflicts" shared by the collective.[10] The congregation also takes time to notice emerging

---

9. White Jr., *Dialogical*, 15.
10. White Jr., *Dialogical*, 17.

themes or to name intriguing feelings. This exercise invites them to ponder "what God's spirit might be saying."[11]

Declarative

The preacher ends the conversational sermon with a monological or, as White says, declarative move. In these final ten minutes, the preacher is invited to make connections between what was shared by the congregation while also using any research and pieces of the good news they had prepared beforehand. White suggests that the preacher pulls together what God revealed to them and some of what has been revealed in the sharing. From the declarative move, White suggests that the congregation enters a bodily response such as a commitment to obedience, confession, affirmation of faith, or a practice such as communion.[12]

Summary of White's Model

I appreciate this model for dialogical preaching. First, I appreciate the clear steps outlined for pastors and congregations who seek to move out of a forty-five-minute monologue sermon into moments of dialogue. I also appreciate how White describes the moderation work of the preacher, using body language, setting space, and establishing commitments for conversation—all those aspects we addressed in previous chapters that allow for healthy, many-to-many conversations.

However, the pastor's authority as a preacher still leans towards a sovereign, expert model. Notice that before the sermon event, the preacher has already drafted the investigative opening move and, in theory, the closing ten minutes or the declarative move. I have seen many preachers who follow a similar form for dialogical preaching choose to completely subvert, forget, or ignore the contributions and the shared moments of proclamation as they go ahead and preach the sermon that they planned to preach anyway. When a preacher does this, they are not showing that they are practicing holy listening or are open to being transformed in the exchange of experiences and ideas within the congregation. If they aren't careful, they

---

11. White Jr., *Dialogical*, 17.
12. White Jr. *Dialogical*, 18.

offer a monological sermon with the appearance of conversation stuck in the middle. How does that make a congregation feel over time?

A Second Option

In what follows, I will lay out a model for dialogical preaching that integrates Priya Parker's genuine authority and Parker Palmer's development of a community of truth. This preaching aims to move from reliance upon a one-to-many dynamic at the beginning of the sermon into a many-to-many connection. Why? To strengthen the bonds of relationship between humans and God's world through shared incarnational proclamation.

Intentional Invitation

The first move of the sermon is not what happens in the first moments of the Sunday worship service. I want to remind the readers that the best way to prepare the congregation for sermon participation is to cultivate consistent social media (and/or in-person) engagement before and after Sunday worship. I think it is more important to consider the feed-forward model from this chapter than the feedback model for dialogical preaching. Using the feedforward model, the congregation potentially enters the sermon event on Sunday already aware of the Scripture passage, aware of the pastor's initial reactions and reflections to the passage, and if the pastor has already started to offer prompts through social media or other avenues, the congregation may already have some reflections and stories to share in the worship space. In Dan White's model, I do not think there is adequate time for the congregants to reflect deeply on what the pastor has presented in the investigative move. But if we think about the sermon as a process that extends beyond the worship hour, then like Parker's description of a good host whose work begins before the invitation stage, we have already set the expectations for how we will gather on Sunday.

An approach of intentional invitation also requires investment from the congregation. Now we are back to the why of preaching and the why of gathering as the body of Christ around God's living word. The congregation cannot assume a passive spectator posture in the preaching moment. Nor can they plan to arrive on Sunday hoping to win an argument. Suppose a congregation and pastor are looking to move into conversational preaching. In that case, they will need to have a season of conversations as a community to establish a covenant to guide the norms for dialogical preaching. This covenant would be like those made in subreddits and pinned in Facebook groups. They are the norms for participation. You are not invited to the gathering if you do not agree to honor the norms.

Exclusion may make some people feel uncomfortable. Especially Christians who have been wrongfully excluded from congregations because of who they are. However, there is a difference between excluding certain categories of human beings and excluding a human being unwilling to show up in a posture of curiosity and respect for others.

Covenant work must be done in advance rather than tagged onto the very first Sunday a congregation decides to try dialogical preaching. Remember that for most congregations, this is a very new practice. Depending upon the experiences of the generations and a congregation, some people will still need to overcome the feeling of being an amateur when it comes to theology or speaking of God. Their shy souls need to know and trust that they are entering a space with other humans who will do their best to respect and lovingly encounter their neighbor.

A Good Beginning

As a fellow knower with particular expertise from theological education that will benefit engagement with Scripture, the pastor plays an important role at the beginning of the dialogical sermon. While a pastor may have already started hosting the conversation through feedforward engagement, there is always a strong chance that other members of the gathering were not aware of the prompts and posts that preceded the sermon. So, as a good host, the first task for the preacher is to bring the gathering around the particular text or theme that will be the grounds for conversation in the liturgy.

Read the Scripture or Scriptures that we are focusing on as a gathering. You may want to have the Scriptures read not by the pastor but by other members of the congregation. Make sure that you alternate between having remote members of the gathering read Scripture and participate in the liturgy and the people who attend the gathering in the building. Encourage everyone to have the text in their hands, whether on their phone tablet or with a good old-fashioned printed Bible.

Now, go into a move similar to Dan White investigative move. As the preacher, you can use your exegetical skills to humanize the actors in the pericope. Who were they? Where did they live? What was the climate and geography of the place where they lived? What were the challenges of ordinary life in that time? What are the particular dynamics between the people named and unnamed in this text? Add depth to the scene and add complexity so that we are less prone to minimize the humans in the Scripture text for our own purposes. Remember, even the humans in the ancient world will be chairpersons in our homiletical conversation.

Next, don't be afraid to articulate authentically how this text has moved you this week. As Ruth Cohen said, participative leadership requires the host to show up as the chairperson with their thoughts, feelings, and experiences to add to the interaction. Pastors are not unmoved movers. Of course, we will be aware that having the opportunity to speak first and to speak as the pastor may make some feel as if they can't share a reflection that seems different or in contrast to what the pastor has shared. You can name this out loud for the congregation and still invite and encourage them not to censor their inner chairperson, to honestly engage with the text in the community, and to allow there to be difference.

This opening moment hosted by the pastor should last for no more than ten minutes.

Shared Proclamation (dance between I-We-and the task before us)

Now, we move into shared proclamation. I suggest that at least thirty minutes be dedicated to opening the space for shared proclamation in my model. Because we are not a chill host, we have arrived with at least three prompts to guide the conversation. We do this with the understanding that sometimes the Holy Spirit moves in mysterious ways. Sometimes, one prompt will be all that is needed. Sometimes, a planned prompt may not fit the moment at all, and we may have to improvise and go with the flow of conversation even if it is not the one we had planned. In all events, it's better to have a plan than no plan at all.

Earlier in the chapter, you saw suggestions for two different three-tiered prompt sequences. Look back at those for reference here. Also, remember our discussions about the work of moderators and hosts in previous chapters. As a generous authority, the pastor will need to be attentive to the conversation, not trying to manipulate or override what is being shared but always trying to 1) keep the congregation focused on the theme and text that is in front of them this Sunday and 2) keep the gathering safe by appealing to the ground rules for conversation that your community has agreed to enact.

As I said before, in the section on Shalom Sunday, you will have to design according to the particularities of your gathering. If you are a congregation with over fifty people in the gathering, then the only way to ensure deep conversation is to train volunteers from the congregation to serve as co-hosts of groups of eight to ten. If you are a congregation that requires splitting off into smaller round tables, then try to set aside time at the end of the thirty minutes to share with the whole group. Again, you can use an app like Mentimeter and other live polling options to project responses that are bubbling up from the prompts for all the congregation to see. And if you are a hybrid congregation, please ensure you have an online host moderating the discussion. Again, find time at the end of the conversation to allow for the hybrid community to share their insights out loud through projection or other creative ways for the good of the whole.

A Good Ending

The key distinction between my model for dialogical preaching and Dan White's is that the pastor does not have the final say at the conclusion of the sermon. Utilizing the flow of Parker's *The Art of Gathering*, a dialogical sermon should be designed so that the one-to-many dynamic at the beginning of the sermon event gives way to a many-to-many dynamic. No one voice gets to have the final word. Instead, we are invited to move in the liturgy from the conversation, allowing the many voices, testimonies, and witnesses shared in the sermon moment to saturate the gathering with no tidy conclusions. And we anticipate that the Holy Spirit of God will work wonders through the conversation and continue to deepen our bonds to one another, the world, God, and concern for God's world.

Like White, I suggest that a bodily response is the best move from the dialogical sermon into the rest of the liturgy. And you may be asking yourself, how can we have a bodily response if we are an online or hybrid worshipping community? But I hope that by now, as we approach the final paragraphs of this book, you remember that people who are at home and online are still people with bodies. They are real human beings. From wherever they are, they can be invited into a bodily response. As the pastor and community, it is up to you to be intentional and creative with how you invite bodily responses. How can we all gather around a table as a hybrid community? If we continue to do our ministry as a hybrid church, what technological tools do we need to increase the many-to-many connections of our hybrid congregation? If we are an in-person congregation, what is the most meaningful physical way to gather around Christ's communion table? You each will choose your adventure as you move forward with the Gadfly.

DEVELOPING PROMPTS FOR FEEDBACK ON CONVERSATIONAL PREACHING

Most rubrics for sermon evaluation exist to support the efficiency of monological sermons. Because of this, the feedback is primarily isolated to an individual sermon as an isolated event. The aspects of reflection matter (exegesis, theology, contextuality, meaningful illustrations, clarity, delivery, etc.), but they center on the agency of the preacher in the sermon event.

Leo Hartshorn noticed this in his essay "Evaluating Preaching as a Communal and Dialogical Practice." Hartshorn, a minister for the Mennonite Church USA who also teaches Anabaptist history, invites us to revise our sermon evaluation tools to "align with" an "emerging understanding of preaching as a church practice."[13] He claims that evaluating sermons by an individual pastor in isolation reveals an ecclesiology in which it is assumed, "1) [there is] a sharp division between clergy and laity; 2) preaching is the sole responsibility of the pastor of a congregation; and 3) laity are passive recipients of preaching."[14]

As more churches engage the Gadfly and implement digital-dialogical practices, homiletics must offer more sermon evaluation forms that keep the congregation in mind. Some examples of questions from Hartshorn that move beyond evaluating a stand-alone sermon are:

- Has the congregation been sufficiently taught how to participate in the church's preaching ministry? If not, what can be done to transform the members' hearts and minds toward an understanding and practice of preaching as a participatory ministry?
- Has the congregation ever engaged in actual dialogue during sermon preparation or presentation? How might this be improved in our congregational context?

13. Hartshorn, "Evaluating," 13.
14. Hartshorn, "Evaluating," 19.

- In what ways has the preaching formed, challenged, and confirmed the theology of this congregation?
- What have been some of the cumulative effects of the preaching ministry upon the congregation's mission and its members' lives as followers of Christ? Share some stories and examples.
- Have church members or the church as a whole participated in some form of public action, community ministry, or service to others due to a sermon or sermons over the past few years? What were the connections between sermon and service?[15]

Evaluation prompts can also evaluate the quality of the host's generous authority in preaching.

- How does the pastor set a topic/text before the congregation? Do they get bogged down in the minutiae of the text/topic? Do they offer too little context and background information on the text/topic? Are the people in the pericope or situation presented as humans with their own chairperson?
- Do the prompts from the host generate conversation? Explain your answer.
- Does the host keep the conversation on theme/text? Explain your answer.
- Does the host moderate the conversation, protecting and equalizing the diverse participants? Explain your answer.
- Fill in the blank: As a participant in the sermon, the host (co-host) makes me feel _____.

Preaching assessment tools can include questions about the extent and quality of the preaching ministry exhibits in connecting with issues faced by congregational members and what's happening in the community and world.[16]

---

15. Hartshorn, "Evaluating," 19, 22–23.
16. Hartshorn, "Evaluating," 21.

CONCLUSION

With any choices you make, I hope they will grow from a desire to remain in touch with God-in-community, the holy three-in-one, whose presence is more potent in the gathering than when we are on our own. As we conclude this journey with the Gadfly, here is a summary of what the Gadfly does *not* want for your ministry:

- Spending more money on tools for technology's sake (technophilia).
- Spending more time on figuring out how to be present in person and online if the only one interested/called is the pastor (not sustainable).
- To go after online people to the neglect of those in-person (technophilia).
- To see these ideas of shift as not impacting preaching in the analog church (technophobia or apathy).
- In short, the Gadfly doesn't want you to leap onto whatever movement is trending unless you have mission alignment (*why*) and a team of co-conspirators.

As I say in all my coaching and teaching, you probably shouldn't leap into a total reversal of your preaching style and method with an established congregation in one week. Doing so puts you at risk of pulling a muscle and taking the body out of the game entirely, if you don't mind the sports metaphor. If you are not the pastor, and you grew up in predominately white Christian spaces shaped by print technoculture, you likely grew up being told to sit still and listen to the pastor. You were trained to think that speaking is disruptive and disrespectful in the preaching event, let alone during un-bolded parts of the bulletin. Years of that training cannot be dismantled overnight. It may take time before the congregation trusts their voice again and sees themselves as someone with something valuable to share as testimony about God.

But the stretch is worth it. Buzz, buzz.

I hope you carry what you learned about the role of the pastor as a host and moderator into your preaching. Also, carry what you learned about the value of all Christians learning to not only share their faith (and doubt) with others as an act of shared proclamation. Midwife ways of being human that involve the loving art of generous listening to perspectives that are not ours. Remember, we are humans, co-conspirators made by the same

Creator. When we come together in preaching with postures of gentleness, respect, humility, and love, we will experience a holy shift of our own.

CONVERSATION PROMPTS

1. What is the largest hurdle between you and a more digital-dialogical preaching practice?
2. How does your role in the congregation impact your perceived hurdle?
3. What digital-dialogical sermon preparation practices are possible/effective for your context?
4. What is your biggest takeaway from engaging the Gadfly of social media, X-reality, and generative AI for preaching in this book?
5. See the appendix for a worksheet that will help you and your community implement the insights from this book.

Appendix

THE ART OF SETTING GOALS
(WITHOUT THROWING YOUR BACK OUT)

My hope is that every congregation/person who reads this book is discerning a learning goal for themselves out of the material.

That said, we aren't always the best at setting good goals for ourselves. How do we define a good goal? Great question. It is highly contextual and so absolutely not a one-size-fits-all situation. I am not offering a list of goals in this appendix for you to take up and apply. Instead, you need to do the work of scanning your assets, gaps, and purpose in the time and place you are in before pinning down a goal together.

Where do goals go wrong?

They throw your back out. Or they don't challenge you at all.

Let me explain.

I know the book medium is a disembodied form. You aren't hearing my voice, seeing my face, as you read these words. You don't know that I am a former athlete (twelve years of soccer) now academic and mother of two approaching her fortieth decade.

I decided out of COVID that I wanted, no, *needed*, to commit to my physical well-being again. I'd made these commitments before with varying degrees of success. Before kids, I successfully signed up and trained for a half marathon. During the season of raising kids, I saw the goal to do Yoga at home three days a week and failed. I also tried running again, with a post-children, six-years-older body, and threw my back out, thereby physically feeling worse than I did before and completely helpless to follow through on care for my body.

What were the attributes (including my changing body) that I needed to consider before I started working toward my post-COVID physical care

Appendix

goals? For one, I realized that the difference between my successful half-marathon training and my failed attempt to run again six years later was more than the physical changes my body endured. Rather, the first experience was a team experience. I was training and raising money for a cause and loved the accountability of the group. Then, some clear aha moments began to bubble up for me. *Casey, you are an extrovert! Solo exercise may not be your thing! You were on a team for twelve years and never complained about the exercise! Find a team to be held accountable by.*

So, I found a group (in barre of all things!). Then, I also found good coaches/teachers who led our exercises, again, harkening back to soccer and the idea that I respond well to someone showing me the way toward achieving my own personal goals within the group. In my late thirties, my soccer body (including a lingering hip injury) cannot make the moves like a twentysomething former dancer can. If I were to try to imitate them, I'd do more harm to my body than help. And my coaches remind me of this with no shame. How? They do their best to keep me in the strengthening zone—that magical space of stretch in between stasis and stress that only leads me to throwing my back out. I still walk away from these workouts sore—this is a sign, after all, of forming new strength in my muscles. But there is a difference between a growing pain and being laid out on your back for a week. A good goal keeps you moving, stretching, and passing through growing pains toward a goal together without taking you out of the game.

In the handbook, conference, podcast, and ministry coaching industry, we can easily miss our contextual strengthening and stretching zone by either:

1. imitating exactly what so and so first church does in such and such a town and expecting to see the same results in a totally different climate, or,
2. being too overwhelmed by the options, never sticking with one, and dwelling in stasis instead.

If you've made it this far, I assume you all are looking to set goals for yourselves in the strengthening/growing zone. Congratulations! Here are some suggested prompts for your conversation on which goal(s) to set for engaging the Gadfly and why.

Appendix

- **Stasis.** Start by describing your stasis/comfort zone with technology. This can be done on an individual level for each participant and broadly done for the congregation as a whole. What technological tools are you using, and feel that you all can manage? How is preaching interacting with the Gadfly of new social media? Take an audit of the congregation's online and social media presence. What do you all observe?

- **Stress.** You could also start with what in this book has caused your heart rate to increase and your muscles to strain? This is where we reflect on the areas of engaging the Gadfly that border on throwing our backs out, that may be too much at this time. Again, discern a response for yourself as an individual and for the congregation. Share these responses without shame and see what emerges in the congregation.

- **Stretch.** With stasis and stress before you, dare to dream of actions for the stretching space that place you somewhere in-between as individuals and a group. Always use your local *why* to confirm the goal(s) that you commit to for a set duration of time before another round of assessment is necessary.

Working together in the stretch zone leads to strength. And it will also eventually lead to new goals because we will find that our congregational body is more capable of engaging the Gadfly after a season of new practices than it was a year before!

Appendix

ENGAGING THE GADFLY GOALS WORKSHEET

Fill in the blank

What is the current why behind the ways you and your congregation engage technology and new media for preaching?

_____
_____
_____
_____
_____
_____

Stasis: At this point, audit your engagement with technology and new media for preaching. Take note of anything, including the use on online, podcast, or social sites for sermon preparation, the congregation's current new media presence, technology utilized on Sunday, etc.

Stress: Now audit the points of unease that emerged from this book and/or the conversations your congregation is having with this book. What right now feels like a move that might throw your back out as an individual? As a congregation? What can you pinpoint as exercises that you might be able to try someday but not in this season?

Stretch: Here is the fun part. And you may want to answer the question below before articulating here the movements you are just a bit uncomfortable with but feel compelled to try as an individual/community.

_____
_____
_____
_____
_____
_____

What people do you need to achieve the goal(s)?

Appendix

_____
_____
_____
_____
_____
_____
_____

What tools do you need?

_____
_____
_____
_____
_____
_____

What training do you need?

_____
_____
_____
_____
_____
_____
_____

Appendix

What accountability plan do you need?

_____

_____

_____

_____

What is the emerging *why* behind the ways you and your congregation plan to engage technology and new media for preaching? This is your purpose power, which can go a long way on those days when you feel sore and ready to go back to stasis.

_____

_____

_____

_____

Plan to proceed. You may need to work backwards together from the goal(s) toward starting steps.

We are planning to:

_____

_____

_____

_____

Because:

_____

_____

_____

_____

Appendix

Steps:

- _____
- _____
- _____
- _____
- _____

Anticipated obstacles:

- _____
- _____
- _____
- _____
- _____

Bibliography

Adichie, Chimanda Ngozi. "The Danger of a Single Story." Video, TEDEd, October 7, 2009. https://ed.ted.com/lessons/TXtMhXIA.
Allen, Jeff. "How Communities Are Exploited on Our Platforms: A Final Look at the 'Troll Farm' Pages." October 4, 2019. https://s3.documentcloud.org/documents/21063547/oct-2019-facebook-troll-farms-report.pdf.
Allen, O. Wesley, Jr. *The Homiletic of All Believers: A Conversational Approach to Proclamation and Preaching.* Louisville: Westminster John Knox, 2005.
Allen, Ronald J. "Some Issues for Preaching in the Future." Academy of Homiletics Annual Meeting. Austin, Texas, 2011.
Andrews, Dale P. "New to Whom?" *Homiletics* E-Forum, Academy of Homiletics (Fall 2006). www.homiletics.org.
Appleton, Maggie. "The Garden." https://maggieappleton.com/garden.
Arthur, Charles. "How Laptops Took Over the World." *The Guardian,* October 28, 2009. https://www.theguardian.com/technology/2009/oct/28/laptops-sales-desktop-computers#:~:text=In%20the%20US%2C%20laptops%20first,years%20earlier%2C%20in%20May%202003.
Baer, Drake. "The 'Filter Bubble' Explains Why Trump Won and You Didn't See It Coming." *The Cut New York Magazine,* November 9, 2016. https://www.thecut.com/2016/11/how-facebook-and-the-filter-bubble-pushed-trump-to-victory.html.
Barna. "A New Chapter in Millennial Church Attendance." August 2, 2022. https://www.barna.com/research/church-attendance-2022/.
Bar-On, Reuven. *Bar-On Emotional Quotient Inventory: Technical Manual.* North Tonawanda, NY: Multi-Health Systems, 1997.
Bass, Diana Butler. *Grounded: Finding God in the World—A Spiritual Revolution.* New York: HarperOne, 2015.
Bell, Karissa. "MIT-Designed Chrome Extension Fixes Your Twitter Filter Bubble." *Mashable,* February 7, 2017. https://mashable.com/article/twitter-flipfeed-extension.
Brooks, Gennifer Benjamin. *Good News Preaching: Offering the Gospel in Every Sermon.* Cleveland: Pilgrim, 2009.
Caputo, John. *Philosophy and Theology.* Nashville: Abingdon, 2006.
Carr, Nicholas. *The Shallows: What the Internet is Doing to Our Brains.* New York: Norton, 2010.
Caulfield, Mike. "The Garden and the Stream: A Technopastoral." Opening keynote for dLRN, Stanford University, October 16, 2015.

Bibliography

Centers for Disease Control and Prevention. "Life Expectancy in the U.S. Dropped for the Second Year in a Row in 2021." August 31, 2022. https://www.cdc.gov/nchs/pressroom/nchs_press_releases/2022/20220831.htm.

Cheong, Pauline Hope. "Authority." In *Digital Religion: Understanding Religious Practice in New Media Worlds*, edited by Heidi A. Campbell, 72–87. New York: Routledge, 2013.

Choudhury, Nupur. "World Wide Web and Its Journey from Web 1.0 to Web 4.0." *International Journal of Computer Science and Information Technologies* 5:6 (2014) 8096–8100.

Clayton, Philip. "Theology After Google." *Patheos*, February 15, 2010. https://www.patheos.com/resources/additional-resources/2010/02/theology-after-google.

———. "Theology & the Church After Google." *Trip Fuller*, April 19, 2011. https://trippfuller.com/2011/04/19/theology-the-church-after-google/.

Cobb, Jennifer J. *CyberGrace: The Search for God in the Digital World*. New York: Crown, 1998.

Cole, Neil. *Organic Church: Growing Faith Where Life Happens*. San Francisco: Jossey-Bass, 2005.

Coleman, Beth. *Hello Avatar: Rise of the Networked Generation*. Cambridge: MIT Press, 2011.

Columbia University Libraries. "Flying Writings." *Wild Boar in the Vineyard: Martin Luther at the Birth of the Modern World*. https://exhibitions.library.columbia.edu/exhibits/show/martin-luther/flug.

Cooke, Bernard J. *Ministry to Word and Sacrament: History and Theology*. Philadelphia: Fortress, 1976.

Craddock, Fred B. *As One Without Authority: Revised and with New Sermons*. St. Louis: Chalice, 2001.

Curnock, N., ed. *Wesley's Journal*. New York: Philosophical Library, 1951.

Daniell, David. *William Tyndale*. London: Yale University Press, 1994.

Deardoff, Darla K. "The Identification and Assessment of Intercultural Competence as a Student Outcome of Internationalization at Institutions of Higher Education in the United States." EdD diss., University of North Carolina, 2004.

De Certeau, Michel. *The Practice of Everyday Life*. 3rd ed. Berkeley: University of California Press, 2011.

Dillinger, Katherine. "Surgeon General Lays Out Framework to Tackle Loneliness And 'Mend The Social Fabric Of Our Nation.'" *CNN*, May 2, 2023. https://www.cnn.com/2023/05/02/health/murthy-loneliness-isolation/index.html.

Dingle, Shannon. "Quitting Online Church is Abandoning the One for the 99." Religion News Service, February 2, 2022. https://religionnews.com/2022/02/02/quitting-online-church-is-abandoning-the-one-for-the-99/.

El-Bermawy, Mostafa M. "Your Filter Bubble is Destroying Democracy." *Wired*, November 18, 2016. https://www.wired.com/2016/11/filter-bubble-destroying-democracy/.

Fazackerley, Anna. "AI Makes Plagiarism Harder to Detect, Argues Academic—In Paper Written by Chatbot." *The Guardian*, March 19, 2023. https://www.theguardian.com/technology/2023/mar/19/ai-makes-plagiarism-harder-to-detect-argue-academics-in-paper-written-by-chatbot.

Fearing, Franklin. "Social Impact of the Mass Media of Communication." *Teachers College Record* 55:10 (1954) 165–91.

Bibliography

Ferrando, Francesca. "Posthumanism, Transhumanism, Antihumanism, Metahumanism, and New Materialisms: Differences and Relations." *Existenz: An International Journal in Philosophy, Religion, Politics, and the Arts* 8:2 (Fall 2013) 26–32.

Gaarden, Marianne, and Marlene Ringgaard Lorensen. "Listeners as Authors in Preaching: Empirical and Theoretical Perspectives." *Homiletic* 38:1 (2013) 28–45.

Geraci, Robert M. *Virtually Sacred: Myth and Meaning in World of Warcraft and Second Life*. New York: Oxford University Press, 2014.

Gould, Meredith. *Social Media Gospel: Sharing the Good News in New Ways*. 2nd ed. Collegeville, MN: Liturgical, 2015.

Graves, Mike. *Table Talk: Rethinking Communion and Community*. Eugene, OR: Cascade, 2017.

Grieshaber, Kristen. "Can a Chatbot Preach a Good Sermon? Hundreds Attend Church Service Generated by Chatgpt to Find Out." Associated Press, June 10, 2023. https://apnews.com/article/germany-church-protestants-chatgpt-ai-sermon-651f21c24cfb47e3122e987a7263d348.

Gupta, Anika. *How to Handle a Crowd: The Art of Creating Healthy and Dynamic Online Communities*. New York: Simon Element, 2020.

Hao, Karen. "Troll Farms Reached 140 Million Americans a Month on Facebook Before 2020 Election, Internal Report Shows." *MIT Technology Review*, September 16, 2021. https://www.technologyreview.com/2021/09/16/1035851/facebook-troll-farms-report-us-2020-election/.

Hardt, Hanno. *Myths for the Masses: An Essay on Mass Communication*. Malden, MA: Blackwell, 2004.

Hartley, John. "Before Ongism." In *Orality and Literacy*, 30th-anniversary ed., xi–xxvii. New York: Routledge, 2012.

Hartshorn, Leo. "Evaluating Preaching as a Communal and Dialogical Practice." *Homiletic* 35:2 (2010) 13–23.

Hinter, Regina, Theo Middelkoop, and Janny Wolf-Hollander. "Participative Leadership." In *Handbook of Theme-Centered Interaction (TCI)*, edited by Jochen Spielmann et al., 171–76. Bristol, CT: Vandenhoeck & Ruprecht, 2017.

Horsfield, Peter. *From Jesus to the Internet: A History of Christianity and Media*. Malden, MA: Wiley Blackwell, 2015.

Howe, Reuel L. *The Miracle of Dialogue*. New York: Seabury, 1963.

Hu, Krystal. "ChatGPT Sets Record for Fastest-Growing User Base." Reuters, February 2, 2023. https://www.reuters.com/technology/chatgpt-sets-record-fastest-growing-user-base-analyst-note-2023-02-01/.

Ingram, Stephen. *Organic Student Ministry: Trash the Pre-Packaged Programs and Transform Your Youth Group*. St. Louis: Chalice, 2015

Ives, Eric. *The Reformation Experience: Living Through the Turbulent 16th Century*. Oxford: Lion Hudson, 2012.

Jenkins, Henry, et al. *Confronting the Challenges of Participatory Culture: Media Education for the 21st Century*. Cambridge: MIT Press, 2009.

Keller, Catherine. "Introduction: The Process of Difference, the Difference of Process." In *Process and Difference: Between Cosmological and Poststructuralist Postmodernisms*, edited by Catherine Keller and Anne Daniell, 1–29. Albany: State University of New York Press, 2002.

Bibliography

Kelly, Samantha Murphy. "Real Estate Agents Say They Can't Imagine Working Without Chatgpt Now." *CNN Business*, January 28, 2023. https://www.cnn.com/2023/01/28/tech/chatgpt-real-estate/index.html.

Kim, Jay Y. *Analog Church: Why We Need Real People, Places, and Things in the Digital Age*. Downers Grove, IL: InterVarsity, 2020.

Kim, Matthew D. *Preaching with Cultural Intelligence: Understanding People Who Hear our Sermons*. Grand Rapids: Baker Academic, 2017.

Kleiman, Glenn. "Teaching Students to Write with AI: The SPACE Framework." *Medium*, January 5, 2023. https://medium.com/the-generator/teaching-students-to-write-with-ai-the-space-framework-f10003ec48bc.

Knight, Kimberly. "Sacred Space in 'Cyber Space.'" *How Firm a Foundation: Churches Face the Future*. Yale Divinity School, Fall 2009. https://reflections.yale.edu/article/how-firm-foundation-churches-face-future/sacred-space-cyberspace.

Kranzberg, Melvin. "Technology and History: 'Kranzberg's Laws.'" *Technology and Culture* 27:3 (July 1986) 544–60.

Lorenz-Spreen, P., Mønsted, B. M., Hövel, P., and Lehmann, S. "Accelerating Dynamics of Collective Attention." *Nature Communications* 10(1) (2019). https://doi.org/10.1038/s41467-019-09311-w.

MacFarquhar, Larissa. "Chimamanda Ngozi Adichie Comes to Terms with Global Fame." *New Yorker Magazine*, May 28, 2018. https://www.newyorker.com/magazine/2018/06/04/chimamanda-ngozi-adichie-comes-to-terms-with-global-fame.

Martin, Ralph P. *Worship in the Early Church*. Grand Rapids: Eerdmans, 1964.

McClure, John S. *Mashup Religion: Pop Music and Theological Invention*. Waco, TX: Baylor University Press, 2011.

———. *Other-wise Preaching: A Postmodern Ethic for Homiletics*. St. Louis: Chalice, 2001.

———. "The Practice of Sermon Listening." *Congregations* 32:1 (2006) 6–9.

———. *The Roundtable Pulpit: Where Preaching and Leadership Meet*. Nashville: Abingdon, 1995.

McClure, John, Ronald J. Allen, Dale P. Andrews, L. Susan Bond, Dan P. Mosely, and G. Lee Ramsey Jr. *Listening to Listeners: Homiletical Case Studies*. St. Louis: Chalice, 2004.

Moiso, Aimee C. "Standing in the Breach: A Relational Homiletic for Conflicted Times." PhD diss., Vanderbilt University, 2020.

Nash, Jay B. *Spectatoritis*. New York: A. S. Barnes, 1938.

The New York Times. "Our Strategy." March 24, 2022. https://www.nytco.com/press/our-strategy/.

O'Hara-Devereaux, Mary. *Navigating the Badlands: Thriving in the Decade of Radical Transformation*. San Francisco: Jossey-Bass, 2004.

O'Lynn, Rob. *Digital Jazz: Preaching, Media, and Technology*. St. Paul: Working Preacher, 2023.

Ong, Walter J. *Orality and Literacy, 30th-anniversary ed*. New York: Routledge, 2012.

Open AI. "Does ChatGPT Tell the Truth?" 2024. https://help.openai.com/en/articles/8313428-does-chatgpt-tell-the-truth.

———. "Terms of Use." January 31, 2024. https://openai.com/policies/terms-of-use/.

Palmer, Parker. *The Courage to Teach: Exploring the Inner Landscape of a Teacher's Life*, 10th anniversary ed. San Francisco: Jossey-Bass, 2007.

"The Papal Belvedere." Wikimedia Commons. https://commons.wikimedia.org/wiki/File:The_Papal_Belvedere.jpg.

BIBLIOGRAPHY

Parker, Priya. *The Art of Gathering: How We Meet and Why It Matters.* Cleveland: Pilgrim, 2018.

Perrigo, Billy. "AI Chatbots Are Getting Better. But an Interview with ChatGPT Reveals Their Limits." *Time,* December 5, 2022. https://time.com/6238781/chatbot-chatgpt-ai-interview/.

Peterson, Eugene H. *The Message.* Bible Gateway, April, 5, 2024. https://www.biblegateway.com/passage/?search=john%3A%201%E2%80%935%3B.

Pew Research Center. "Mobile Fact Sheet." January 1, 2024. https://www.pewresearch.org/internet/fact-sheet/mobile/.

———. "World Wide Web Timeline." *Feature,* March 11, 2014. https://www.pewresearch.org/internet/2014/03/11/world-wide-web-timeline/#:~:text=World%20Wide%20Web.-,1993,flourish%2C%E2%80%9D%20Wired%20later%20writes.

PolitEcho. "Is Your News Feed a Bubble? Find Out How Polarizing the Content on Your News Feed Is When Compared to Your Friends As A Whole." https://politecho.org/.

Postman, Neil. *Amusing Ourselves to Death: Public Discourse in the Age of Show Business.* London: Penguin, 1986.

Priests for Equality. *The Inclusive Bible: The First Egalitarian Translation.* Lanham, MD: Rowman & Littlefield, 2007.

Randolph, David. *The Renewal of Preaching.* Eugene, OR: Cascade, 2009.

Reid, Clyde H. "Preaching and the Nature of Communication." *Pastoral Psychology* 14 (1963) 40–49.

Reklis, Kathryn. "X-Reality and the Incarnation." New Media Project at Christian Theological Seminary, May 10, 2012. http://cpx.cts.edu/newmedia/findings/essays/x-reality-and-the-incarnation.

Rose, Lucy Atkinson. *Sharing the Word: Preaching in the Roundtable Church.* Louisville: Westminster John Knox, 1997.

Rubner, Eike. "Shadows." In *Handbook of Theme-Centered Interaction (TCI),* edited by Jochen Spielmann, et al., 228–32. Bristol, CT: Vandenhoeck & Ruprecht, 2017.

Senn, Frank C. *Christian Liturgy: Catholic and Evangelical.* Minneapolis: Augsburg Fortress, 1997.

Scharer, Matthias, and Bernd Jochen Hilberath. *The Practice of Communicative Theology: An Introduction to a New Theological Culture.* New York: Herder & Herder, 2008.

Shirky, Clay. *Cognitive Surplus: How Technology Makes Consumers into Collaborators.* New York: Penguin, 2010.

Sigmon, Casey T. "Failure to Discern the Online/Hybrid Body: A Captivity of the Eucharist." For the special issue of *Currents in Theology and Mission: Eucharist and Online Worship: Toward Extended Theological Reflection* 50:1 (2023) 13–18.

———. "Preaching by the Rivers of Babylon: How an Exile from Pulpit and Pew Can Change White Preaching on the Other Side of the Pandemic." *Interpretation: A Journal of Bible and Theology* 75:2 (2021) 123–33.

———. "Reaching out for Community in a Digital World: Problems & Possibilities." *Word and World: Solitude and Community* 42:2 (Spring 2022) 164–72.

Simard, Suzanne. *Finding the Mother Tree: Discovering the Wisdom of the Forest.* New York: Alfred A. Knopf, 2021.

Simson, Wolfgang. *The House Church Book: Rediscover the Dynamic, Organic, Relational, Viral Community Jesus Started.* Carol Stream, IL: Tyndale, 2009.

Smith, Dennis E. *From Symposium to Eucharist: The Banquet in the Early Christian World.* Minneapolis: Fortress, 2003.

Bibliography

Sperber, Werner. "Structure – Process – Trust." In *Handbook of Theme-Centered Interaction (TCI)*, edited by Jochen Spielmann et al., 165–70. Bristol, CT: Vandenhoeck & Ruprecht, 2017.

Spiers, Elizabeth. "I Don't Have to Post About My Outrage. Neither Do You." *The New York Times*, October 17, 2023. https://www.nytimes.com/2023/10/17/opinion/social-media-israel-palestine.html.

Stevenson, Dwight E. *Disciples Preaching in the First Generation*. Nashville: Disciples of Christ Historical Society, 1969.

Stewart, Teresa J. *The Small Church Advantage: Seven Powerful Worship Practices that Work Best in Small Settings*. Knoxville, TN: Market Square, 2023.

Suchocki, Marjorie. *The Whispered Word: A Theology of Preaching*. St. Louis: Chalice, 1999.

Suttle, Tim. *Shrink: Faithful Ministry in a Church-Growth Culture*. Grand Rapids: Zondervan, 2014.

Trust, Torrey. "AI & Ethics." Slide deck licensed under CC BY NC 4.0. https://www.slideshare.net/slideshow/ai-ethics-presentation-by-dr-torrey-trustptx/267039022.

Turkle, Sherry. *Alone Together: Why We Expect More from Technology and Less from Each Other*. New York: Basic Books, 2011.

———. *Reclaiming Conversation: The Power of Talk in a Digital Age*. New York: Penguin, 2015.

van Dijck, José. *The Culture of Connectivity: A Critical History of Social Media*. New York: Oxford University, 2013.

Vodafone. "25 Years Since the World's First Text Message." December 3, 2017. https://www.vodafone.com/news/technology/25-anniversary-text-message.

Voelz, Richard W. *Preaching to Teach: Inspire People to Think and Act*. The Artistry of Preaching Series. Nashville: Abingdon, 2019.

Warren, Tish Harrison. "Why Churches Should Drop Their Online Services." *The New York Times*, January 30, 2022. https://www.nytimes.com/2022/01/30/opinion/church-online-services-covid.html.

Weiser, Benjamin. "Here's What Happens When Your Lawyer Uses ChatGPT." *New York Times*, May 27, 2023. https://www.nytimes.com/2023/05/27/nyregion/avianca-airline-lawsuit-chatgpt.html.

White, Dan, Jr. *The Act of Dialogical Preaching: The Convergence of Conversation and Proclamation in Public Discourse*. Self-published, 2024.

White, James F. *A Brief History of Christian Worship*. Nashville: Abingdon, 1993.

White, Susan J. *Christian Worship and Technological Change*. Nashville: Abingdon, 1993.

Whitehead, Alfred North. *Adventures of Ideas*. New York: Free Press, 1967.

———. *Process and Reality: An Essay in Cosmology*. New York: Free Press, 1972.

Yale Youth Ministry Institute. *Dr. James K. A. Smith on Cultural Liturgies* Video, YouTube, August 8, 2018. https://www.youtube.com/watch?v=LO4IdsJsPv0.

Yang, Sunggu A. *Digital Homiletics: The Theology and Practice of Online Preaching*. Working Preacher 14. Minneapolis: Fortress, 2024.

Zsupan-Jerome, Daniella. *Connected Toward Communion: The Church and Social Communication in the Digital Age*. Collegeville, MN: Liturgical, 2014.

www.ingramcontent.com/pod-product-compliance
Lightning Source LLC
Chambersburg PA
CBHW020848160426

43192CB00007B/833